One baby, one scared young mum, would she hurt her child? A social workers account. Read on to find out

CHAPTER ONE

'Is that Carey Patterson, social worker?' the voice at the end of the phone asked.

I'd just started work in West Rowbury Child Protection team when I took a phone call. It was 1982, so before the law on taking children into care changed. But the human part of social work is always the same, a mix of drama and compassion. Let me show you.

'Caz, my name is Carey, but people call me Caz. How can I help?' I asked.

'Phew! Thank goodness. Detective Sergeant Sheila Murray here,' I could hear the sigh of relief in her voice. 'I've a young woman and her baby here with me, she's gone to the loo now but she's quite upset. I've seen her a couple of times lately and I'm really concerned about both of them.'

'Why is that?' I asked. It was my turn on duty that day. That meant answering the phone and dealing with anyone who rang in and didn't have an allocated social worker to help them. Duty always keeps you on your toes, you never knew what was coming in next. 'Tell me more.' I sat back and listened.

'She's called Kirsty Burton and she's 19, her baby is Craig and he's around ten weeks old. She came in to ask about violent partners a couple of weeks ago,' Sheila explained. 'So I took her somewhere quiet for a chat and made her a cup of coffee. She was asking if the Police could help when the person you live with gets violent and starts hitting out. So we sat and talked about domestic abuse for a while.'

I could guess the way this conversation was going, and it wasn't good.

'Well, the more she talked the more tearful she got. I asked did she want to tell me about any particular event, thinking its about her and her boyfriend who she lives with. But she said no. I thought at the time and still do that she was talking about herself but she insisted she was talking about someone else. There's not much you can do without a proper, formal statement of complaint, so I let it go.'

'People often do sound others out when a relationship is going wrong don't they?' I reflected. 'It sounds like she's testing the water, feeling like she ought to leave her partner but isn't ready yet.'

'I agree.' I confirmed. My colleagues told me Sheila did a lot with women of all ages. Coupling compassion with a hefty dose of common sense, everybody liked her.

'Anyway, she came in again and asked more or less the same thing so we had another long chat, she had no bruises and said she was talking about a friend. But the thing is she's come in a third time and now both she and the baby have bruises.

That rang alarm bells in me. 'Crikey. Whereabouts?'

'Craig's is on his forehead, Kirsty's is a black eye, and the area around her jaw and her lip is swollen. The thing is, I know Kirsty's partner Trevor Johnson and he is bad news. They live with him although the baby is not his. Kirsty moved in with him about three or four months ago. Trevor was bought up by his nan and when she died he took over the tenancy on her flat. When Kirsty first came in to the station I was asked to talk to her because it's my sort of thing, I know the area and the families in it having been bought up here. She looked really weak, tearful and pale and she was shaking like a leaf. Apparently Trevor threatened to hit her during an argument although she denies he actually hit her.'

'Gosh, how awful for them.' These sort of referrals always got my adrenaline flowing because its down to me to keep the baby safe, and the mother if possible.

'Well, she insists the bruises are nothing to do with her partner. And apparently the baby didn't witness anything because there was nothing to witness. But I don't believe that for one minute. Kirsty says a tin of talcum powder fell on the baby after his bath and it's nothing to do with the boyfriend. But I know Trevor's family. They've a long standing feud with several other gangs, they're always falling out and fighting, but in reality they're all just as bad as each other. Trevor is showing every sign of being like his dad, he's already got convictions for assault. He's got the gift of the gab though, he could charm the stars out of the sky. But with a history like that, I'm worried that he may hit the child again, and next time it could be worse.'

'That is really bad news,' I sympathised. There are some things that will alert a social worker straight away and a conviction of assault in someone who has access to a baby, plus an injury and a parent who isn't protecting the child will always be a concern. 'Does Kirsty have any family that can help look after them so she can leave Trevor?'

'Kirsty doesn't see her own mother, she was always drunk from what she tells me.'

'Does Craig have any family that could look after him for a while? Like a dad?' I asked.

'I don't think so,' Sheila thought a moment then answered. 'I don't know anything about his dad, I don't think he's on the scene though.'

This was not sounding good. 'Have you spoken to her about safety with Trevor around?'

'I've done that several times,' Sheila explained with a note of exasperation in her voice. 'She doesn't see a problem and quickly backtracks anytime I mention violence.'

'Sounds like we might need to move the child if Kirsty's not willing to look at risk, doesn't it?' I mused, thinking out loud. 'If that's the case we'll need a Place of Safety Order.'

The law is different now, police can make an Emergency Protection Order so you don't need a magistrate but in 1982 when this happened you did. The human situation never changes though. 'I'll need to speak to my boss about it, but given the evidence, I can't see any alternative.'

'Me neither. I'll give her a coffee and a quiet place to talk. Could you join us?' Sheila asked. 'If she's still with Johnson and planning to take the baby home to him, I can't see any alternative to taking the child away can you?'

'No, I agree. We can't stop her risking her life, but we can keep the baby safe. I'll be with you as soon as I can. I'll just discuss it with my boss then we'll probably have to get someone to arrange the Order, assuming my boss agrees.'

'Of course. And if you don't get the order, depending which of our surly old magistrates is on today, I'll be taking that child home with me. Sod my career!' Sheila laughed.

I knew her reputation well enough to know she was just using that to emphasise how serious she was about needing to protect Craig. I didn't believe she'd act on it. On the outside she was as tough as old boots, but inside she had a heart of gold. You just wouldn't want to mess with her.

'Ok then,' Sheila's voice changed. 'I can hear her. She's coming back now so I'll have to go.'

I checked our social services records to see whether we'd seen this woman and her baby before. But we had nothing on record and a quick phone call to the health visitor confirmed they'd had no particular concerns when they'd seen Kirsty shortly after Craig was born. That is often the case with first babies, there isn't any history because there are no school records or nursery reports so you have very little background information to go on.

I discussed the matter with my Practice Supervisor, Graham Hoyle, the next person in the chain of management above me, now that I'd done all the background research.

'We will need a Place of Safety Order on this child, assuming he has no family on his dad's side to help,' he agreed. 'The child isn't safe with Johnson and Kirsty is not willing to accept that he is a danger to either herself or Craig. She's not protecting either of them. You go to the station and talk to her about her awareness of Trevor's violent behaviour and check on possible paternal family help and I'll find a magistrate and ask for a Place of Safety Order. Also let the hospital paediatrician know we need to bring a baby in and why. He might need treatment. Oh, and one other thing, ring the fostering team and ask if they have a placement available and book it.'

'Ok I'll do that. In what circumstance won't we need the order?' I hadn't been qualified that long and often asked the more experienced team members for their advice.

'If she accepts Trevor is a danger and lets us take him into care or comes with him,' Graham checked his briefcase as he spoke. 'Or has a suggestion of a safe place to take Craig, maybe a family member.'

I suppose I should have guessed that I thought. 'How long will you be?' I asked. A case like this is always a big responsibility and every fibre of my body was eager to make sure the process was right and as smooth as possible for everyone.

'An hour or so, hopefully less,' Graham explained quietly. 'I think I know which magistrate is on duty today and that will make me quicker. If not I'll need to ask the legal secretaries to find out who is on duty. Then I'll give the evidence, wait for the order, and rush over to you.' Graham had been qualified and working in child care so long that nothing seemed to phase him. Just speaking to him and hearing his summary of this situation made me feel more in control, because he helped me understand what powers social services could have in each situation. I had been qualified a year, long enough to have done quite a lot of things, but not everything. The experienced social workers on the team were so serene and seemed able to deal with whatever came in. I knew that's how I wanted to be.

'Any tips on how to manage the family?' I asked.

Graham grabbed his coat, but he slowed to explain as he put it on. 'It may well be a highly charged emotional experience for them. Both mother and son are bound to be tense and fretful so listen a lot and ask lots of open questions. You can't lie about our worries or trick her into thinking we're there for something else. But whatever happens this won't be the last time mother and son see each other, it's probably going to be the start of a long process. But you will be with the police and I'll be there to actually enact the order, if we need it,' Graham explained in his usual calm style. 'How does that sound to you?'

'Great,' I nodded, feeling much more in control.'

'See you in a while,' Graham opened the door and left.

I nodded agreement as he hurried away.

Becky, my colleague and friend, had got the idea that I was about to do something difficult probably from hearing scraps of conversation. She was busy on the phone and had been for a long time. That is standard practice in our office, it's always madly busy. But she threw me a supportive smile and a big thumbs up. I thanked her and left the office, grateful that Graham had laid out the steps I needed to take so clearly.

The police station was an old Victorian building right in the centre of town, part of the same building as the town hall. Once proud and clean, it was now grubby and dingy. I took the steps two at a time eager to save that baby and I reached reception as fast as possible. The place seemed empty. Once in, I pressed the bell, resisting the temptation to keep ringing it, and waited.

Nothing happened. The whole area was as quiet as a grave. I was totally alone except for an old tramp dozing off in a corner.

I hit the reception bell again. Still nothing.

I craned my neck to look into the back room, hoping to find a receptionist or anyone I could explain my plight too.

I was almost tearing my hair out with images of that baby needing help in my mind when at last someone emerged from a backroom, walking slowly towards me her mouth full of something she was chewing. She wiped her hands on her skirt before she reached me. I willed her to hurry and explained my purpose as fast as possible. I was given instructions to go right to the top floor, where Sheila would meet me.

The stairs were open on one side looking over the ground floor foyer. The higher up the stairs I got the darker it became. The large downstairs windows were replaced with a few smaller ones, too high and grubby to look out of. The whole atmosphere at the top was gloomy, even on a sunny day. Officers had long been hoping for a new station but successive governments had been and gone without any money having been invested in the place.

I went through the double doors at the top of the stairs and stopped at a door that had a big handwritten notice on it saying, 'Please do not enter,' but I knocked on the door anyway, as I had been told. It was opened almost immediately by Sheila who I recognised from having seen her briefly before, in uniform her expression unusually tense.

'Ah Carey, thank goodness you're here.' She pulled the door a little behind her, and whispered to me. 'Have you got the order yet?' I could hear the tremor of nerves in her voice, unusual for Sheila.

'Graham is asking for it now.' I replied feeling on edge almost. I'd learnt like most social workers that no matter how concerned you were inside, it was much more useful to keep at least an outer veneer of calm. Being stressed yourself always made things worse and this situation was difficult enough in the first place.

'Good.' Sheila visibly heaved a sigh of relief and waved me inside towards a chair. 'Come on in. Meet Kirsty and Craig.'

I looked over at the mother and son sitting in the office and said 'Hello' trying to hide the shock I felt on meeting the pair. I could see the bruise on Kirsty straight away, I couldn't miss it. Purple, fresh and right in her eye socket it stood out like a beacon against her pale white skin. She looked at me from beneath a long fringe, her expression blank, almost as if hoping she wasn't part of this world. The child was whippet thin, with hollow cheeks, dull eyes and a bruise on his forehead too. Most babies, whatever their skin colour, have soft skin with a peach-like surface. Craig's face looked grimy and sallow, his gaze tense and fearful.

I'd never seen a baby look so traumatised.

I introduced myself with a smile. It didn't go down well. Suddenly, something seemed to hit Kirsty, she stood up grasping the child tighter without hugging him to her, he just hung awkwardly over her arm as she took a step towards the door.

'You're a social worker?' she growled. 'Let me out of here!'

Craig looked confused and puzzled. He began to cry, a weak, thin, thready noise, as if he was scared and unsure whether to cry or not. He didn't look to his mother for comfort, it was as if that hadn't occurred to him. That seemed to me to say a lot about the bond between the couple. Kirsty pulled the baby to her, not in an affectionate way, more using him as a shield, ensuring we wouldn't be able to take him from her.

'Sit down,' Sheila said in quiet, soothing tones.

Kirsty took a step towards the door. 'No. I'm going!' she shouted.

I stood, but the policewoman was closest and moved her ample frame to bar the woman's way. 'No, don't do that,' she soothed in her soft Irish lilt, putting a calming hand on the woman's arm. 'Sit down and

7

listen to what we have to say. We've something we need to talk through with you.'

'What!" Kirsty glared daggers at us, looking from one to the other of us in fear. 'So you can take him away from me? Is that it? Not so bloody likely!'

'Hey, Kirsty, it's not like you think,' I added, sitting down myself and patting the empty chair next to me, inviting her to sit, hoping that my calm action would inspire peace. 'Let me explain.'

My heart pounded in my chest. I could see Kirsty was on the verge of leaving.

I had to come up with something to delay her right now. I kept up my peaceful tone. It wasn't easy, I was scared for the duo myself. 'I can see that bruise you have to your eye.' I pointed to it. 'It looks really sore.' I didn't hold back. I let her see my concern in my facial expression. 'It really should be seen by a doctor, it might damage your eyesight.'

She stopped, and listened to what I was saying.

'It's only small, I'll be okay,' Kirsty replied, quieter now, perhaps in response to my hushed tones

I looked at the baby more closely. I am no medic, but he didn't look healthy. I felt enough concern about his daily care on its own to want to know more. 'What's this mark here?' I asked Kirsty, pointing at it on Craig's forehead but as my hand drew close he screamed and shouted in fear.

That worried me and I could see similar worries on Sheila's face. How had he learned that hands coming towards him were something to be frightened of? There could be only be one way, but I didn't say anything then because Kirsty would have run away and I needed to find out more. 'I'm sorry,' I soothed, moving my hand away from the baby. 'I won't do that if you don't like it.'

Kirsty turned and glanced nervously from one of us to the other, her gaze quizzing our faces. I tried to read her expression. I saw fear, nervousness, confusion, panic, humiliation, despair, a whole kaleidoscope of feelings, each of them unpleasant.

One thing I was sure of since arriving here was that this baby was in danger and his mother seemed a muddle of emotions and probably wasn't strong enough to protect her son.

Thankfully, gradually Kirsty did sit down. She rested hesitantly on the edge of the chair. The baby seemed soothed too and stopped crying but looked far from relaxed. I smiled over to him and said how sweet he was hoping to ease his tension, but he gave no response. I wondered if there was too much stress in his life for him to have learned to enjoy being spoken to. But either way it gave us space to think for a moment and I was thankful for it.

'Now let me explain why Carey is here,' Sheila said, taking control of the situation and moving a stray lock of hair from her face. 'Don't be alarmed, we're here to talk, that's all at the moment. But there are some things we need to ask you about.'

Kirsty was silent and tense, looking nervously from one of us to the other but she did listen.

'Now, Carey, this young woman is Kirsty and her son Craig, though I'm sure you've already worked that out. She has been to see me a few times now, isn't that right?' Sheila looked at Kirsty for confirmation of her words.

Kirsty frowned, as if uncomfortable with the conversation, but after a second or two nodded dutifully.

'Babies are lovely, but very hard work. We were worried that you look very stressed and wondered how you are coping?'

Kirsty's posture softened a little. 'I do get tired. But I'll cope. I have to.'

'What are your family like? Are they helpful?' I asked, wanting to check in case there was a helpful family in the background.

'Nah.' Kirsty's gaze dropped. 'I don't see my mum, she's not well and drinks a lot. My nan bought me up but she's dead now. There isn't really anyone else.'

'That is so sad for you.' No wonder I had seen despair in her eyes, she really had no-one except a mum who sounded like she needed a mum herself. 'And your dad?'

'I dunno know where he is. I haven't seen him since I was little.' She shrugged her shoulders. 'I'm not really bothered.'

'That is sad. It's tough when you're young and have no family behind you.' So much of life was just chance, some people had wonderful families and some didn't. It seemed to me more down to luck than anything else.

'What about Craig's dad and family?' I asked.

'I don't see him no more.' Kirsty responded brusquely.

'That is a shame for you. You really are are on your own aren't you?' I sympathised.

'Just the way it goes, innit?' Kirsty answered shrugging her shoulders. I could only agree.

'What is your relationship with Trevor like?' I could guess, but I wanted to hear her version.

The reply wasn't so clear this time, and Kirsty seemed to think about her answer. 'Alright.'

9

It sounded unlikely to me, but I let it go.

'I think you met Trev when you were about seven months pregnant.' Sheila interjected. 'Isn't that right?'

Kirsty nodded agreement.

'But there have been a couple of problems in the relationship, especially since Craig was born, I think that's fair to say.' Sheila glanced at Kirsty, as if to be sure she was keeping her attention. Kirsty frowned as if puzzled, but eventually nodded agreement.

'That's a shame,' I acknowledged. Relationships are hard to get right aren't they? As I know from personal experience.' I added a little groan to my last phrase, hoping to build a bond. I sure had had my share of relationship problems. 'Where did you meet Trevor?'

There was silence for a while. Then she spoke tentatively, hesitantly. 'I went out for a drink one day. I was on my own. I got chatting to someone. Trevor,' she explained, as if unsure if she should be saying anything.

'Sounds good so far,' I reassured. 'Did you get on well straight away?'

'Yeah,' she laughed, relaxing a little more. 'I liked him and he liked me. At first he spent a lot of time at my place. Then we decided there was no point paying two lots of rent. So I moved in with him.'

'You were lonely?' I asked. Loneliness can push people into relationships that aren't right for them, I often found.

'S'pose,' was the timid reply.

'We've all been there," I soothed.

'Tell us about Trevor,' Sheila said. 'Did he tell you he has a criminal record?'

'Um, yeah.' Her complexion paled.

'I'm talking about convictions for assault on people? It's not just taking cars or goods. Violent offences. Hurting people.' Sheila spoke with gravity, emphasising the seriousness of the situation.

I could see Kirsty gulp. I don't think she had heard this before even though she said she had.

'There's reasons why these things happen isn't there? There's two sides to every story,' Kirsty sought to justify Trevor's history.

'There's no good reason for anyone being violent to any other person Kirsty.' Sheila said in an insistent tone.

Alarm bells seemed to be going off in Kirsty's head, I could see her tense a little.

'Does he like babies?' I asked.

'S'pose.' Kirsty shrugged her shoulders.

'How does he feel about being a step-father?' I asked, a chill passing over me.

'Yeah, yeah he's alright,' she mumbled, her voice hesitant and shaky.

'That's not what you told me when you were here last week,' Sheila challenged. 'You weren't sure if he even liked kids if I remember right.'

'He was just in a bad mood that day. He's not usually like that.' Kirsty frowned, I could see she was unhappy. 'I can talk him round. It's not a problem.'

'And you've given up your own place already?' I asked for clarification.

'I had problems there.' She frowned and shifted about nervously avoiding all eye contact. 'One of the other tenants knew Trevor and ganged up against him. It wasn't his fault.'

'What wasn't his fault?' Sheila asked looking straight at Kirsty as a headmistress would to a pupil.

'He was accused of nicking things. But I know he doesn't do that sort of stuff.'

This worried me. 'And you have bruises?' I asked.

'I told you,' Kirsty shouted, 'I fell over and hit myself on a table!'

'You told me last week Trevor had threatened to hit you!' Sheila reminded her.

'Yeah, well, I lied, didn't I.'

Kirsty seemed to be getting visibly more tense as she realised she was cornered, both in words and deeds. I was silently begging for Graham to arrive with the Order. I wasn't sure how much longer we could keep Kirsty talking and stop her from running out with the baby. 'And Craig has a bruise?' I asked and looked at him. His sleeve had pulled up in the recent fracas. I could clearly see another bruise on his lower arm. A paediatrician would have to decide how they came about. I looked up at her. It was enough to alert her to my plans. 'I'm worried…' I began. 'I can see another bruise on Craig.'

Kirsty, tense all along, finally snapped. 'Look, I don't have to stay here…' and she got up fast, faster than Sheila this time. Pushing Sheila out of the way with her forearm. Kirsty was through the door, baby flopped over her arm, and out before we could stop her.

I was worried she'd go home with the child and Trevor could be in another bad mood and then…the rest didn't bear thinking about. So we chased her to stop that happening.

Kirsty turned right and ran a few yards along the corridor and through the double doors. She found herself at the end of the balcony beyond which was a dead end with a group of police officers coming up the stairs, possibly on their way to a meeting, and blocking her way down. She was stuck, cornered holding the baby three floors up with Sheila and I in hot pursuit.

CHAPTER TWO

Kirsty paused, looking left and right at the top of the stairs as she checked the way out, which gave Sheila and I time to catch up with her. Sheila got to the stairs first and me slightly after. We barred the way down, which was blocked lower down anyway, by a group of police officers, probably on their way to a meeting or returning from lunch. Sheila was asking Kirsty to come back and talk as I reached them.

'Fuck off out of my way!' Kirsty shouted to Sheila at the top of the stairs, the baby hanging lopsided over her arm. He was crying in what sounded like fear now.

'No Kirsty,' Sheila and I blocked Kirsty's path and we moved with her when she attempted to push past us.

'Kirsty you're not in the right mood to have care of a baby,' I said as I held out my hand. 'We've got a few more things to talk about yet and I can get you some help. Can we go back to the office and talk about this please?'

The commotion had brought out a crowd of people on the floors below, to see what was going on.

Kirsty turned away briskly and tried to walk past me. But Sheila and the other officers, realising something was wrong, barred her way on the stairs making a deep barrier that she couldn't push through.

'Come on Kirsty, let's go back in the office,' I pleaded with her.

'No. I'm not going nowhere near you. I know you're gonna take him off of me!' Kirsty shouted, her body shaking, tension building. 'Out of my way!' She tried to push past Sheila regardless of the barricade of police.

'Kirsty…' Sheila stated, obviously ruffled.

The child lay limply over his mother's arm, as if he was inanimate, like a coat or jumper. He was whimpering, but Kirsty didn't seem to notice.

I was worried about Craig. At his age his back and neck would need more support than he was getting. Discomfort might be one cause of his crying. I stepped forwards, holding my hands out to take him. 'Let me hold Craig if you're going' I said as calmly as possible.

'Get off of him!' she shouted, turning away from me, Craig whisking through the air as his mother turned. Her movement took her closer to the edge of the balcony with a terrifying drop just inches away. He cried louder for a while. His mother still didn't appear to notice her son's discomfort or how near she was to a dangerous drop. 'You're not having him!'

Kirsty was seething with anger, her sole focus was on arguing with me first and Sheila second. I worried she'd do anything to avoid giving the child up and looked at the drop beside her. The thought was a horrific prospect.

I could see everyone else was thinking the same thing, that Kirsty might drop one or both of them over the edge, judging by the tension in their faces. A group of people on the ground floor were looking up at us. They had obviously had the same thought and were gathering in case either of them came over the balcony.

'It's not safe for you or baby to be so close to the edge,' I said calmly, holding my arm out to try and usher mother and baby towards safety.

'Out of my way!' Kirsty shouted, ignoring my arm, pulling Craig away with a jerk and getting even closer still to the edge. 'I'm going. You can't keep me here, I've got rights, I've done nothing wrong and nor has he. Now move! Move!' she barked at Sheila trying to push her aside, but Sheila stood firm.

'You can't take Craig when you're in this sort of mood.' Sheila spoke calmly.

'That's right,' I added. 'We can get his bruise seen by a doctor, and yours if you like. There might be a brain injury that needs treatment, you can never be too sure with head injuries. I'm not happy for him to go home with you. That bruise on his head could have serious consequences. Come with me and we'll get you both seen to.'

'No way!' Kirsty shouted, pulling Craig to her side, away from me and closer to the edge. 'I knew he was what you wanted as soon as I saw you! You social workers are all the same, you're not having him. Pick on someone else! There's nothing up with him. He's perfectly safe. Now out of my way!'

'He's got bruises. They need to be seen by a doctor,' I replied and Sheila backed me up.

'Kid's get bruises. I told you how he got them,' Kirsty argued back in a sarcastic tone. 'Haven't you seen them before? What have you got? A quota of babies you need to take to get promotion, is it? Is that why you want him?'

'That's not true,' I argued. 'We don't have an amount of babies we have to get. The reason I think Craig needs to see a doctor is because the bruise is on his head, near his brain. There's another on his arm. He could have a fracture on his skull or a broken arm and those could cause him long term health problems. I also wonder if someone might have hurt him, maybe the bruise wasn't caused by a talcum powder tub, and how did that one on his arm get there anyway? I want the doctor to check whether he needs treatment. We need to get him checked out, then if we need to find out how they happened or who did it to stop it happening again. You want to know that too, surely?'

'Yeah, well I will stop it happening again right?' She tried to push past us.

'So someone did do them then?' I replied. That made Kirsty furious, the tension in the air was way past boiling point.

No-one could get behind her because she was at end of the balcony. It would take her seconds to turn and throw either herself or Craig or both of them over the side. She was certainly angry enough to do that and heading closer and closer to danger all the time. It seemed as if she'd do anything to stop anyone else getting Craig. I'd seen no evidence that she loved him enough to want to keep him safe.

Quite the opposite. Kirsty seemed like she was in a complete muddle and in denial about the cause of the bruises on her son.

Sheila and I took a step closer to her, ready to grab either if need be, but Kirsty stepped away from us. Graham was nowhere to be seen and without the order I had no authority to take the child from her. But I knew if she put the baby in danger in anyway, we would take the child away from her whatever the law said.

For the time being we had stalemate. We couldn't get near the baby, Kirsty couldn't get past us.

'You're a sensible girl when you're not riled,' Sheila soothed. 'You can see the situation from our point of view can't you? You're not thinking straight. Trevor isn't an easy chap to get on with. You've said that yourself. Why don't you let us take Craig, just while you get yourself sorted out?'

I took up Sheila's point. 'We have some lovely caring foster carers who could help, some of them could even take you too if you like. That would give you a rest and time to think about things. I've helped with some mother and baby placements in the past and they've really worked out well.'

'I said no! Get out of my way!'

Our soothing tones hadn't softened Kirsty. She was bending over now, face contorted with anger, screaming with tears running down her face, completely out of control. 'You're not taking my fuckin' baby! Do you hear!'

'He needs a doctor,' Sheila insisted.

'Come on now, Kirsty,' I took a step towards them. Sheila did the same. Kirsty took a step away from us. We spoke in voices as soothing as we could muster.

'Get away from me!!! I'm warning you! Fuck off the lot of ya!! Just fuck off didn't you hear me!' Kirsty took a step even further back, the baby dangling over her arm and screaming earnestly now. She made no attempt to console him or hug him to her. She seemed to think of him as something like a bargaining chip, a barrier to keep us away from her, she gave the baby no warmth or reassurance whatsoever, despite his distress.

'Craig's crying.' I took a step towards her. Persuasion proving futile. I wasn't prepared to let Kirsty upset Craig like this. 'Let me take him, I'll calm him down, then you can have him back and we can talk about keeping both of you safe.'

I held out my hands and for a moment Kirsty seemed to think about it. I stood patiently, willing her to see sense, but whilst Kirsty was thinking about how to respond to me, Sheila stepped closer.
You could have cut the tension in the room with a knife. Order or no order, that child was in danger and there was no way we were letting him leave this building with his mother.

'C'mon now. That's enough of this nonsense, he's scared. Pass him here!' Sheila stepped towards Kirsty briskly, arms outstretched. But Kirsty moved backwards and turning, lifted the baby up towards the top of the balcony railing!

I heard our audience gasp in fear and Kirsty glanced down to the group beside her!

In an instant Sheila and I lurched towards her. Sheila was closest to the edge of the balcony and grabbed the baby, pushing Kirsty back in the process. I was slightly behind Sheila so grabbed Kirsty round the waist, and pulled her down on top of me to safety. Several other officers dashed forwards and lined the top of the balcony stopping any further movement towards the danger at the edge. I heard gasps and sobs from the audience and Craig was screaming.

'What do you think you're doing?' Sheila said to Kirsty. She was furious understandably and hugged the baby close to her, rocking him from side to side to soothe him. 'You could have killed the pair of you!' I pulled myself up to a sitting position and looked around, to gather my senses. A couple of burly police officers came and asked if I was ok. I was out of breath and couldn't answer, so I just nodded.

Kirsty stood up, lurching towards Sheila's arms. 'Give my baby back! I WANT HIM!!! I WANT HIM! You got no rights to 'ave him!'

'Kirsty, he has bruises. You know he has bruises,' Sheila pointed out, the tension in her voice suggesting she was trying desperately hard not to be angry. 'You have bruises. You were quite clear last week when you said you felt Trevor might hit you. He's dangerous and you don't see it. So how can you protect Craig eh? Answer me that.'

'I was lying… I was trying to get Trevor in trouble. We had fallen out,' Kirsty screamed and stood up. 'Give him to me!'

I stood up. 'Kirsty, even if you hadn't said that Trevor had hit you I still wouldn't be happy for you to have care of Craig. You're too upset. Someone hit you that is obvious to me, and Craig has bruises, and you can only see that you need to be loyal to Trevor,' I explained. 'You've got no other realistic explanation of how Craig's bruises came about and it's not good enough care for him.'

'You got no rights over him!' she screamed ignoring my points and jabbing a pointed finger viciously at me. 'I'm going to the papers and the courts. You'll fuckin' pay for this you bastards!'

I'd heard that line so many times. 'Kirsty, there's not a court in the land who would back you up on that one, bearing in mind what you were about to do to him just now.' My anger was fully justified, but for Craig's sake we needed to be calm. He was traumatised and frightened enough as it was. He needed calm, caring people around him to make him feel safe, and that started with me and Sheila.

'And what was I gonna do then anyway? You don't know do you? I was trying to protect him from you!' Kirsty looked around herself as if seeing everyone for the first time. She looked bemused and dropped her head into her hands and began sobbing loudly. She dropped and sat on the floor looking defeated then, and looked up at me, her gaze empty, her voice mute.

Yet there was something about her I couldn't work out, something about the desperation in her voice. Did she feel out of her depth with a baby? Was a return to single life what was calling her, but she didn't know how to get back there? Was she even ready to be a mother? Either way I felt her pain. I realised I was dealing with not one child but two. I leaned towards her and rested my hand on her arm. 'Would you like to come with us to the hospital doctor?' I asked.

'Are you gonna take him off of me then?' She looked up from beneath an overgrown fringe now sodden with tears, her gaze reflecting a myriad of emotions.

'I don't know,' I admitted. 'But I'm worried enough to take him to a specialist doctor, and if they say he has been hurt in a non-accidental way we'll have to find a place where he is safe. And I can't see how he is safe with you, since you're not clear about how both of you got those bruises. Your partner has got convictions for assault. We need you to work with us to find out how those marks got there, if not by Trevor.'

She shook her head in disagreement.

'If we do insist that he goes into care it doesn't have to be forever', I soothed. 'And there are some foster carers who could take you too. It's called a mother and baby placement, and they can help you learn about looking after a baby. We need you to think of not only of Craig's safety, but yours and not just today, but for the rest of Craig's childhood.'

There was a pause whilst Kirsty was, I hoped, weighing up the situation and our audience listened in silence.

At last she spoke.

'I did think of Craig. He is safe.' She almost spat as she spoke and got up, pushing her way, unimpeded now, past the group to the stairs. The peaceful mood she was in just a few moments ago vanished as suddenly as it had arrived.

I moved out of her way. 'Ok,' I said. 'I want you to know this isn't the end. It's not the last time you'll see Craig unless that's what you want. I'll take him now to a doctor's and then to a foster carer, but I will come and see you later and make arrangements for you to see him if you like.'

'Piss off!' she replied and stomped down the stairs, police officers moving out of her way as she walked.

I watched her as she went. She had stopped shouting now and seemed calmer. But I doubted if she was calm inside. But there was no legal way we could detain her. She hadn't given clear enough signs of possible mental ill heath to be sectioned under the Mental Health Act. She was probably depressed, but not enough to detain her without her consent. She was clear, understood what we were saying and was able to rationally answer back, she was just wrong about her care of Craig. The law can't stop people making what appears to others to be a wrong decision, but it can stop you hurting a child. Kirsty was a young woman in need herself, I suspected although she was over the age of eighteen. You can't force people to work with a social worker, but you can maybe work with them when they're calmer.

We let her leave.

Craig was at last settling, snuggling into Sheila's bosom and reassured by her gentle manner.

My luck changed then. Graham arrived at the back of the group. He looked satisfied and held up a piece of paper to show me, but as he got closer his expression changed to confusion. 'What's been going on here?' He looked around him.

A uniformed officer answered, 'a woman tried to throw a baby and herself over the balcony,' a no nonsense tone to his voice as he walked away.

'Bloody hell!' Graham edged his way towards us.

Many of the bystanders left at this point, presumably to return to their jobs.

'Thank goodness for that!' I said, brushing my clothes down. I could clearly see the document with typed wording in his hands. It said 'Place of Safety Order,' in big letters at the top. That gave us the legal right to take Craig into care. The local authority was now Craig's parents, at least until the order ran out. If it had been refused we'd have had to go back to the magistrate telling him or her about the little scene we'd just been through. There was no way anyone could claim that Craig was safe with Kirsty now.

'Better late than never!' I exclaimed, relief flooding through me.

'Sorry about the delay,' Graham replied, looking a bit guilty. 'I had to wait. The order lasts up to 28 days, but it's good practice to get an Interim Care Order fairly soon if you think you'll need it, because that gives the family some right to challenge us if they want to.

'Good point,' I replied.

'This poor lad must be hungry.' Sheila rocked the child and walked towards us. 'Why don't we let Caz take him now? It feels to me like he needs his nappy changed, and he must be starving hungry.'

'That's a good point,' I said moving towards Craig. There were no facilities to change or feed a baby in a police station of course, so I had to take him as he was. Our next stop would be the hospital doctor, then Craig's new temporary home. Foster carers are used to taking babies in really difficult circumstances, such as in the night, not knowing what to feed them or when. They accept that in these emergency situations parents don't often pass on these details. He seemed calmer now the commotion had eased. 'Are you coming with me little one?' I asked, holding my arms out to take him to the car. Thank goodness that Val, our admin person, had had the foresight to remind me to take the office baby car seat with me. I guess she had a hunch I'd need it.

We reached the hospital after a few minutes. We were to meet Consultant Paediatrician Dr Marianne Gladstone in the children's out patients department. I had met her in the course of our work several times. Almost as soon as I had reached the waiting room, the doctor came to greet us.

'Hello,' Marianne smiled as we approached.

Craig didn't respond but looked dull and gloomy in the bright, cheerful surroundings. We walked into the consulting room.

'This is the young man I was telling your staff about,' I held him in his car seat towards the doctor. 'I don't know when he had his last feed or what brand it was, his mother was in no mood to tell us.' I felt the damp patch on my tee shirt, where I'd hugged Craig close to me on our way to the car. Getting close to people who haven't been well cared for is one of the perils of the job. I had had nits and scabies before when there had been no choice other than to get close to others who had been unable to take care of themselves.

'Oh dear. We'll take him into a side room.' She led the way to a small room with a desk, some chairs and an examination bed in it. There were coloured posters and toys everywhere to help keep a child occupied, but Craig took no notice. She flicked a switch inside as we entered. 'I have a bottle and a clean clothes ready that I got from the ward. I had a feeling he might need it. We keep a box of clothes ready for just this sort of emergency. You can return them when you've finished with them.'

'That is good to hear.' I lay the child gently on the couch and stood by him to make sure he didn't fall off. 'I'll make sure the clothes are returned.'

'Since he's not screaming with hunger, I'll examine him and change his clothes to make him more comfortable. He'll take his feed better that way too.'

'Good point,' I agreed. 'I suspect they have been on him far too long.'

Marianne gently undressed the little chap, chatting and talking to him the whole time. Then she began moving his nappy gently. It didn't come away easily, it needed gentle tugs. The skin was red and sore and Craig cried when it was pulled away, though Marianne was very gentle.

'He also doesn't look around him as a baby his age would. He's kind of distant somehow,' I said.

'That could be a sign of emotional numbness. Our profession is just beginning to understand that babies who have had a bad start in life do show signs of emotional trauma. Previously it was thought that they were too young for events in their life to show up in their behaviour. New research is now showing that is not the case,' Marianne cleaned Craig's nappy area as she spoke.

'Even at that young age?' I queried.

'Yes. Amazing as it may seem, even tiny babies can show signs of emotional distress in various ways.'

'I suppose it makes sense when you think about it.' I mused. 'Ok, I could see Kirsty was probably depressed, it is all too easy especially when you're young, to get yourself deep into a really difficult situation with a violent man, I've seen so many people who've done that. But how could you let your child get as poorly as this? Maybe going to the police was Kirsty's way of admitting something was wrong and hoping they would take action? I think that some parents wanted their child taken away from them or other help but can't admit it, so they create circumstances where they won't be able to keep them. I guess when the child is older if he or she finds their parents, should the separation be final, they can say it wasn't their fault and blame the social worker.'

'I agree with you there.' The doctor turned to Craig's bruises.

'There are bruises on his arm. Look here. Marianne pointed to Craig's arm to show me those that had peeped out from under his sleeve. 'I suspect someone has held his forearm so tightly they have left a mark, you can see one bruise here and there are corresponding marks on the other side of his arm which would indicate a grip injury. It is tender when I touch it. You can see him wince in pain when my fingers go anywhere near it.'

Marianne demonstrated and Craig did wince and I winced in sympathy. Then the doctor searched all over his body, making a methodical assessment of his eyes, hips, heart and genitals to check his condition. After a while she stood back and moved the stethoscope away from her ears to her neck. At first she said nothing, and I felt the nerves in my tummy pulling with concern.

'He's underweight and very small for his age. She looked straight at me, her tone serious. 'This child has suffered non-accidental injuries, in my opinion. He has a bruise here on his forehead which I don't believe was caused by a talcum powder container. It would't be heavy enough and I can see it was quite a hefty blow. Also the mark on his arm is probably that of a hand which has grabbed him, you can see the marks clearly. I'm sure both are non-accidental injuries.' Marianne showed me using her own hand to demonstrate the placement of the fingers.

'I see what you mean.' I could almost cry at hearing a child this young and lovely had been so badly treated. But as a social worker you soon learn to let your feelings take second place, all your attention goes on changing things for the children you are working with.

'So far he looks quite a bit behind normal development. He isn't looking around him with the curiosity many babies show at this age,' Marianne continued. 'But since we don't know where his mother was at in her pregnancy when he was born, it's hard to tell if that's normal or not. Obviously pregnancy is usually nine months long but if babies are born early, say at seven months, then they do take that bit longer to catch up. It also looks to me like he's not used to having people talk to him,' Marianne said. 'He gives no awareness of anyone holding him or talking to him. You'd expect some feedback, a glimmer of recognition or similar, from a child his age.'

'I was thinking the same myself,' I agreed. 'We've just spent a couple of hours at the police station and he was the same. He didn't seem to acknowledge anyone who was holding him there either.'

'It's worrying. The lack of eye contact is a concern and some reactions I tested were defiantly slower. He may have some sort of learning difficulty, or it could be lack of attention at home,' she explained, fastening his clothes.'I suppose only time will tell the exact cause of his problems.'

Who could do that to such a young child? Trevor Johnson, I thought, then reminded myself to keep an open mind in case it was someone else.

Craig whimpered feebly, he didn't seem to like being dressed. 'Sorry, sorry, darling,' Marianne soothed. 'Let me just get you all cleaned and sorted.'

It wasn't long before he was cleaned up and put in fresh clothes and his nappy area was bathed and cream applied to his sores. All this done, he looked more comfortable. 'I thought we'd give him a bottle now and he can arrive at his foster carers with a full tummy. He'll bond with them quicker if he's not hungry,' Marianne said. 'I don't think he needs anymore physical treatment at the moment other than nappy cream. But I would like to see him again to gain some clarity on his mental health.'

Craig took the bottle she gave him. It was nice to see him eating and clean but it made little difference to his mood. He still didn't give eye contact or take an interest in his surroundings. But at least he was safe now.

'I'm pleased his injuries haven't caused greater problems. He is going to lovely people. Janet Marsh and her family, the fostering and adoption team told me.' I knew the Marsh's from previous placements. 'She and her family have been fostering for years, they love babies and all muck in together.'

'I know Janet,' Marianne said, taking the empty bottle away and sitting him up to burp. 'She's often bought the children she looks after in to see me.'

The wind obliged and Craig did a big burp. We had done our best for him now, only time would tell how he'd be long term. But at least he would get proper treatment from now on.

'There you are love, that's you fed now.' Marianne lifted him and held him so he was looking straight at her on a level with her gaze. 'You're all sorted and ready for your next big adventure aren't you?' She looked directly at him with a smile and a cheery face. He still didn't respond.

With a slight air of disappointment, Marianne lowered him into the car seat. 'I'll need to see him in a fortnight. If you or Janet ring my secretary she'll give you an appointment. Meanwhile his bottom will need dressing with the cream I'm about to give you at each nappy change. His bruises don't need any treatment, I don't think there are any underlying physical issues, like broken bones or similar. But he clearly has been grabbed too tightly, poor sausage. I'll draw the placement of bruises on a chart, no doubt you'll need a copy of that and my report for court.'

'Yes,' I replied with relief picking up the car seat. 'He is on a Place of Safety order now and we will be applying to the court for a full Care Order.'

'It goes without saying that you have my full support in that, and thank goodness you have him safely so no future harm can come to him.' Marianne opened the door for me.

I nodded in agreement and took Craig back to the car for the next stage in his journey.

Often people had said to me they don't know how you could take children away from their parents. But looking at the reality of some children's lives, I don't know how some people can think it's a problem. It's hugely rewarding to move children somewhere they will be loved and looked after if you can see that their current situation is leading to harm.

But taking a child to someone they've never met before must be very traumatic for them. How would Craig deal with that I wondered, as I drove off.

CHAPTER THREE

'We're taking you to a foster carer called Janet. You'll like her and she'll love you,' I explained to Craig as we drove to her house. I knew he was too young to understand what I was saying, but I hoped my words were soothing. Not that he needed much in the way of reassurance, he seemed very peaceful and contented, quite an easy baby to look after now he had been fed, changed and was in peaceful surroundings.
It took just a few minutes to get to Janet's and I parked outside her large house. Most foster carers have big houses because they need to have spare bedrooms. Part of me felt that many of the people struggling with their parenting hadn't had the best chances in life. They often had small housing, unhelpful families and poor resources all round.

Janet must have been waiting, she opened the door quickly.

"Hello,' she said walking towards me. 'So this is the young man who is coming to stay.' She lifted him out of the baby seat and we went into her kitchen. It was warm and welcoming with a big Aga giving out heat and a gorgeous smell of cooking. A lot of people that come to social services say that no wonder their children do well in care when they come to places like this with every comfort you could want. That made sense. It seems to me that the more resources you have the easier life is, though money doesn't solve every problem.

We sat at the kitchen table whilst I explained Craig's recent history, since that was all I knew. I said we'd been to see the paediatrician and reported what Marianne had said and the need for a new appointment, and the cream for his bottom.

'Well, you're here now, little man,' I said to Craig allowing him to hold my finger, which he did without hesitation. That was a reflex action that all young babies have and it was a good sign.

'I think you and I are going to get on very well, aren't we?' Janet addressed Craig directly. She had a gift with babies and hugged him close to her. 'His poor mother must have been in quite a state herself.'

'She was,' I agreed. 'But hopefully I can help her too.'

'So we have you all cleaned up?' Janet soothed. 'That's good. And now we'll keep you like that.'

The baby looked up in response to her eye contact and rubbed his eyes with his tiny fists. His fingers looked slim, not like the fat, chubby fingers with little dimples that most babies have. 'He doesn't look at you and smile like other babies do,' I explained. 'The doctor thought

24

that might be a sign of problems of some sort, but it's too early to tell yet. Doctors are only now beginning to research trauma in babies.'

'You poor wee thing,' Janet consoled. 'We'll get you all sorted out here. You must be exhausted. I have a bed ready for you in a quiet corner of the kitchen, so I can keep an eye on you while I finish cooking.'

I watched in delight as the picture of humanity at its best unfolded in front of me. This woman, whose children had all grown and left home, would do her best for him, a total stranger. I knew that whatever he needed, food throughout the night, cleaning, unconditional love, he would have it. He would have her total devotion, supported with love and care by her own family.

Janet knew that she would have to give him up one day. She had told me on many occasions that she couldn't do long term fostering because, being that bit older she couldn't commit to a full eighteen years. Sometimes she cared for parents with their child, and there were plenty of families that needed her care.

I saw Janet had everything ready, a crib in the corner, a box of toys, a changing area a short walk away. She lay Craig down on the crisp white sheets in the bassinet. He seemed tiny, a pale, weak, a little mite lost in the crib. But at least he'd stopped crying now. I'm sure the tension in the police station would have disturbed him and hopefully he'd be more relaxed now he was away from that. It made me think of how much stress there can be in the home of a child and how it affects them even if they're not directly involved in it.

'Have a good sleep, love,' Janet said as she covered Craig with a blanket.

At the moment Craig's future was uncertain. He'd probably go back to his birth parents or a relative or possibly some other complete stranger if he was going to be adopted. Janet's work was a selfless gift of love that she had given to many, many children throughout her life, and would continue as long as she was able.

It was a benefit that Craig's mum may never have had. No wonder she struggled to be a mother, she really needed a mother herself. The child had been neglected and maybe not given regular food but I guessed his mother was so depressed she had struggled to care even for herself never mind for a baby. What she needed was help rather than criticism. I hoped she'd work with me and we could change things for both of them.

'As you know, we should have a formal placement meeting with his parents right now, to arrange contact and visits from relatives and so on. Obviously we can't do that at the moment,' I explained. 'But we can do the part of the form that gives you his details in case you need them in an emergency.'

'That is very helpful,' Janet agreed. 'It is always different for each child and it's useful to have the details just in case I need to show police or out of hours social workers.'

'Of course.' I took the form and details from my briefcase and began writing. 'I'll leave a copy with you and fax this to the out of hours team in case they need it. The master copy will stay on his file in our office. We won't allow any contact here or any visits from parents or other relatives who may make themselves known. This address must be kept secret because Kirsty's partner has a history of violence. I can discuss that when I find Kirsty, but all contact and meetings will be at the family centre, at least for the time being. Are you happy about that?'

'Yes, for now,' Janet agreed. 'I will rethink that if circumstances change.'

I completed the rest of the form with what we knew of his medical and social history and quickly wrote out a copy for Janet.

I left the pair shortly after having satisfied myself that Craig was in the best hands possible and with a promise to set up the placement arrangements and complete the paperwork with Kirsty.

Craig we could sort out and he was fine where he is now, but where was Kirsty? She looked to me just an older version of her son tense, rootless, unsettled. I guessed she yearned for love herself and was looking for it in all the wrong places, from people who weren't into giving but taking big time. I thought Kirsty probably needed to learn to value herself before she was able to choose a partner who would look after both her and her child. But I knew it wasn't easy to change the way you looked at life.

I suspected I was looking at an adult with an attachment disorder, someone who desperately wanted to be loved, someone who would care for her. Someone kind-hearted, honest and worthwhile, but with little experience of this in her own life, she chose the wrong people.

Often, at the core, at the heart of this problem was the total conviction sufferers often have that they aren't worthy of decent love, of having a person in their life who would love and care for them, day in, day out. Without help, Kirsty may well be destined to repeat a pattern that was familiar to her, that was predictable, safe, habitual even if unhealthy.

She might see all around her good, loving relationships where there was plenty of love and care. But she would recoil from these like a cat from water. She could wrongly believe they weren't for her, that they were too good for her. They might feel completely alien, that she simply wasn't good enough for them.

It would be lovely if we could help her out of that destructive spiral of belief and set her up in a place of her own with Craig, maybe with the help of foster care for herself, and the support of the local Family Centre who would guide and nurture her as long as she needed it.

Whatever Kirsty's problems, she deserved to know that her son was safe and that she'd be able to see him at a contact centre if she arranged it with me. I decided to pop in and see her on my way home. Could I change Kirsty's future?

Or was her past on repeat play?

With Trevor's history of violence and the news that his girlfriend's son had been taken from her that could possibly provoke a violent reaction from him if I were to go to Kirsty's house alone. So I stopped at the police station to ask for an escort.

They agreed to send two officers to meet me outside Trevor's block of flats, in the car park. If Kirsty chose not to engage with me, well, at least I had tried. I would continue offering.

It has always been the case that police and social workers work together on child protection cases so the police can deal with the criminal issues and social workers can deal with the welfare issues. It would be the child protection police who would be working with me on the case to work out who was responsible for Craig's bruises but since they weren't available today the usual uniformed officers were with me. They never interfere with social workers by questioning or our decisions, they were simply there for our safety.

As the doctor was sure Craig's bruises were not accidental, the Child Protection unit would be following up the injuries from their end to find and prosecute whoever was responsible for hurting Craig. It was easy to think it was Trevor, but it could have been someone else and at this point we had to keep an open mind until the investigation was complete.

I pulled up outside the tower block known as River House. The flat was on the fourth floor. To say the whole estate was shabby was an understatement. Weeds grew from the cracks in the pavement, the cladding was cracked and falling from the building. One end of the the nameplate 'River House' had come away from the wall it was supposed to be attached too. It was hanging, from one screw, riddled with grime and had become faded over the years.

The social work team and I were often on the estate, as were the police, dealing with the problems of too many people without resources living too close together. Wealthy people often had big gardens as well as large houses for youngsters to play in riding bikes, making dens, or hide and seek. They could afford trips to the swimming pool, horse riding, theme parks and any sort of entertainment.

But not those who lived on this estate.

The council had built a park nearby for small children but it would be too far to walk for many and really only offered a handful of things like swings, slides and roundabouts which many of the young people had long outgrown. Supervision was necessary for all but the oldest of children. It must be so depressing to live here, I thought, and badly though some people behaved my heart went out to them suffering the continuing onslaught of grinding poverty and grim housing. A good clean and a lick of paint would have gone a long way towards cheering the place up but the council chose not to spend the money on it so it felt like the whole place was just a warehouse for keeping poor people in, out of the way of everyone else. Those who were able could train at the local college to gain better employment. Those who for whatever reason didn't want that sometimes found work in the few local businesses. Some who weren't able to do that had to put up with the hand they had been dealt in the uneven circumstance of life.

As I arrived I saw Constables Bob Morris and Nancy Turner waiting outside for me in a marked car. They greeted me warmly, we had worked together on a number of cases. The local police were the one bright spark in a dearth of local public services. Wherever possible they tried to work with people, not against them, and it softened all but the hardest criminals.

We walked towards River House together. A group of teenagers loitered in the stairwell of one block we had to pass on our way. They gave us a thorough look over as we got closer, one of them flicking a lighted cigarette end towards us. I couldn't tell if it was meant to touch us or not but thankfully it didn't. Bob shouted over to the lad he thought was perpetrator and said 'Oi,' in a stern voice, pointing his finger at the offending item. The lad muttered 'sorry,' and we carried on our way.

Groups of teenagers like that never worried me. I had spent much of my youth hanging around in a similar gang and I'd learned to recognise that the menacing look on their faces was usually just boredom and trying to look tough.

There was a different set-up for unemployed people when I was young. I had been able to attend a job creation scheme, whereby local charities were commissioned to take young people on jobs that otherwise wouldn't get done. Mine was with an archaeology group.

That had given me the start up into higher education and work that I needed.

We reached the stairwell and were greeted by a whirlwind of old sweet wrappers, dirt and other rubbish that didn't bear closer inspection. We didn't try the lift, knowing from previous experience that it usually stunk and had a tendency to break down. The stairs had the advantage that you weren't going to get stuck in a little metal box if the lift developed problems, but the stairwell wasn't pleasant either. I didn't like to rest my hand on the banister as I usually did for balance, it looked so grimy. The walls were covered with old chewing gum, smears of dubious origin and graffiti, some of it very artistic. But there were also plenty of lewd comments, presumably about local people, and phone numbers to ring to get things that…, well, let's just say weren't available elsewhere.

I was exhausted by the time I'd reached the fourth floor. Goodness knows how I'd have coped if I had small children to look after or even worse, had to get them up the stairs with me.

Eventually we reached Trevor's front door. I wanted to tell Kirsty that in the doctors opinion Craig's bruises were not caused in the way that she had described and that the cause of these hadn't had a feasible explanation. Therefore he was in our opinion at risk at home and would stay in care so we could ensure his safety and the Police child protection team would investigate thoroughly.

I'd also need to ask more about his dad, since whether Craig's dad knows about him or not, as a parent he did have rights and we'd need to involve him and possibly his family, especially if we went ahead with the Care Order.

There was also the matter of the Child Protection Conference. In 1982 social services had a child protection register, a list of all children in that area which a child protection conference, a meeting of those professionals working with the family, deemed at risk. It was a quick way for schools, family centres, GP's etc who could ring to see if a child was on that list and therefore at risk. Then any concerns about them would be escalated.

Then someone begun a register of sex offenders some years later and people got concerned if anyone mentioned a child that was on the register, because it was so easy to mix the two up, since both of them were known as the register. So now the child protection register has a different name. It's called being on a child protection plan. It doesn't trip off the tongue so easily, but it still does a vitally important job. Both Kirsty and Craig's dad would need to be invited and have a chance to read and comment on the report I would write to be circulated to the conference attendees. That didn't mean that I would have to change what I had written to Craig's family's liking, unless I had made a mistake, but that I would add their comments to my own, if we disagreed.

On that cold March afternoon I knocked on the door, concerned since I didn't know what sort of response I'd get but reassured by Bob and Nancy two paces behind.

I knocked and waited for a reply. I'm sure I heard something inside, but couldn't be sure. I thought I could see the figure of someone inside through the frosted glass of the front door. Whoever it was was bigger than Kirsty, so it was probably her boyfriend Trevor. Whoever it was didn't walk to the door, but stood listening. I knocked again, just in case they hadn't heard me the first time but nothing changed. The person didn't move. After a few minutes they turned and went away and the sound of the TV was turned up.

'I don't think you're going to get an answer.' Nancy stepped forward and looked through the frosted glass with me. 'We might as well go. But we'll come with you tomorrow if you like?'

'If you wouldn't mind,' I gratefully accepted their offer. We agreed a time and I put a note in the letterbox on a compliments slip with a calling card in an envelope. I always kept some stationery in the back of my diary so I could leave notes for people when they were out. Putting it in an envelope kept it confidential.

I wanted the note to be friendly, but not too friendly, so I wrote,

'Dear Kirsty, I popped round today to tell you that Craig has settled into his foster carer well. We will need to have a meeting so that we can discuss things and make arrangements for you to see him, if you want. I'll visit at 2pm tomorrow to see you or you can phone or see me at the office below if you can't make this appointment.

Yours, Carey Patterson, Social Worker.'

I gave the number of our out of hours duty service so that she could ring them to ask how Craig was if she wanted to, put it in an envelope, sealed it up and pushed it through the door, happy that I had done my utmost to keep Kirsty involved in Craig's life even if she chose not to take me up on it. I imagined she'd be pretty down now, but you can't always be sure.

I didn't know Kirsty well enough to know what was behind her recent behaviour. In my mind it could be that she was depressed, possibly with post natal depression. Although the two illnesses share similar names they are very different. Post natal depression occurs in the year after a woman gave birth. But a more general type of depression could be for different reasons. It wasn't long ago that some research had identified some risk factors for depression in mothers. That could have affected Kirsty's bond with her son. Depression might also be behind her choice in partner, maybe she was so low she was easy prey for someone who was looking for a relationship but maybe was not willing to put his partner or her child's needs first.

It might also be that Kirsty was simply too young to have a baby, not physically of course, but mentally. Being a parent meant a massive change in lifestyle. Kirsty was only 19, the age at which most young people are out having a good time and making some sort of start in the world of work. Maybe she resented Craig for the demands he made on her. New babies were certainly exhausting, many people when new to parenthood are shocked at the amount of work one very small child could make and the effort it took to look after them.

All of these issues would need to be looked into. I'd need to be sure Kirsty's depression couldn't be treated or managed in some way that didn't mean she'd lose Craig before we went for a full care order.

But meanwhile whatever Kirsty's background, I'd have to navigate that most difficult of relationships, having removed someone's child yet needing to get the best out of them. Only then would they have maximum chance to get their child back if that was what the parents wanted, and most importantly of all, in the child's best interests.

CHAPTER FOUR

'Oh there you are,' my colleague Becky welcomed me on my return to the office the next morning. 'Graham said you'd had a really intense day yesterday.'

I threw my bag on my chair as I reached my desk. 'You can say that again! I was helping a woman and child who was so angry, it looked like she was going to throw her baby off the high balcony in the police station.' I was eager to talk, to be quite honest. The whole incident had left me unsettled and I couldn't speak to my husband Fas, Fasil, about it because it was confidential. But obviously I could at work. Sharing details about clients sometimes helped manage the inevitable emotional consequences on staff.

'Oh gosh that's scary. I wouldn't want to witness anything like that,' Becky sympathised.

'Me neither.' But I was puzzled. 'You learn all these things at university about deprivation and attachment disorders yet when you meet someone who might suffer with something like that they seem so normal.'

'That's how it is,' Becky laughed. 'People suffering with these things don't have a sign showing their problems, you have to work it out for yourself. Sometimes with the help of a colleague. How did it make you feel?' she asked switching her tone to one of care. 'Taking someone's child can be one of the most stressful things in this job.'

I screwed up my face in contemplation. 'Confused, if I'm honest. There was no way Kirsty could look after that baby at that time, that's for sure. She was so angry, the most angry I've ever seen anyone, and nudging towards the edge of the balcony with Craig in her arms. I wouldn't have been surprised if either one or both of them had gone over. Yet I can't hate her or feel cross with her for it. But I feel I should be angry with her.'

'That is normal. I feel for you, working with angry people isn't easy at the best of times,' Becky soothed. 'Really you were working with two children, not one weren't you? That's why you're not angry with Kirsty, because she's really just a child herself in a situation she doesn't know how to deal with.'

'Yes, that's it!' Suddenly everything made sense. 'Kirsty might be physically old enough to have a child. But she's not mentally is she?'

'That's right. It's quite common. Sometimes if someone hasn't had a good childhood themselves they haven't learnt how to care for a child and they struggle. How is the baby?'

'I'd never thought of childhood as a way to learn about childcare but I guess it is. Craig he's called, and he's really sweet, but he looked totally bemused and anxious yesterday.' I paused and thought about my answer. 'Its hard to really say how he is. His bruises will heal soon, the doctor was sure about that. But as to his weight and mental condition she wasn't so sure. He's underweight and weak. The doctor said that could be the result of trauma, but it also might indicate some sort of underlying problem.'

'That's about right,' Becky agreed. 'It often does take time for the full extent of the damage to be known, but he is in the best place now. Anyway, you look to me like you're in need of a cuppa. Want one?' Becky picked up my mug and shook it to emphasise her question.

'Yes and yes please! I got home so late last night I'm still exhausted, but it was so worth it. I stayed for a while to help Craig settle in with Janet. When I left he was starting to relax and snuggled right up to her   .'

'Janet is great with babies, she'll have him settled in no time.' Becky had been qualified a few more years than me and was a font of wisdom in all things social work. She'd explain things in a nice, easy manner. You never felt daft for having asked questions. Come to think of it, my whole team were like that. I was really very lucky.

I was halfway through my tea and Becky and I were going through the messages and letters that had arrived for us over the last 24 hours when our Team Manager, Trish Green, Graham's boss, summoned me into her office. It was uncommon enough for anyone to get a Place of Safety Order and I guessed it would be about that so I wasn't unduly worried. Trish was always so supportive as we all tried very hard to do our best.

'Ah, Carey,' she swivelled round in her chair to face me as I walked in. 'Take a seat and tell me all about your day yesterday. Graham tells me you had a difficult time.'

'I did.' I perched on the seat she indicated and went through the events of the day before, recounting the drama in the police station, taking Craig to hospital, then to foster care and so on. It took me a good ten minutes till I'd finished, '...so that was about it really,' I concluded.

Trish kept her gaze on me the whole time, the warmth in her eyes filling me with pride that I had done a good job.

'Graham said it got very tense. I must say I thought you dealt with it very well. I was speaking to a senior police officer yesterday afternoon and he was singing your praises too,' Trish enthused.

I thought I was going to burst with pride! 'Thank you,' I muttered.

'What did Marianne Gladstone say about him?'

'She said his bruises are clearly non-accidental, though they aren't serious and will heal. But he is very thin and weak. She wasn't sure if that indicated some sort of condition or if it's a result of his life so far.'

'The other thing is how well is Kirsty?' Trish looked at me puzzled. 'You probably haven't had time to think about that, but it is something to bear in mind, it makes a big difference to case planning.'

'I guess it must,' I summarised my thoughts of yesterday to Trish.

'Time will be needed to fully understand Craig and Kirsty, won't it?' Trish replied. 'Now, have you thought about long term planning for Craig? We have plenty of people who are happy to adopt a child with special needs, if it comes to that.'

'I haven't had time to do any planning,' I admitted. 'I suppose he'll stay where he is until we see if Kirsty is going to look after him? I went to see Kirsty yesterday to talk about it with her but I couldn't get a reply, though I thought I saw someone inside.'

'That is worrying.' Trish's brow furrowed. 'There are many families who make it difficult to work with them. But I guess you spent all your energy taking him to safety yesterday.'

I nodded agreement. Trish was right, she seemed to easily remember what her own early days as a social worker were like and offered just the right amount of support, not enough to stifle you but just enough make you feel confident in what you were doing. I loved that. We all did.

'Don't forget to arrange the Placement Planning meeting with Graham, the foster carers, yourself and Kirsty. You might need to include any close relatives that are in Craig's life if there are any. That's where you can agree on contact, who will see Craig, for how long and where, plus any day-to-day issues like when the Health Visitor calls, whether family can see him, that sort of thing. We review it often, especially at first, so we can make any changes that we need without too much delay.'

'I see what you mean,' I said, quickly jotting down notes in my diary. There was such a lot to think about and do in this job I had quickly learnt that it was too easy to forget something really important unless you wrote it down.

Trish waited for me to catch up until she carried on. 'Now, as I see it, there are two ways forward for this lad,' she continued. 'Either his family need to learn to care for him properly and that does not include partners with any sort of violent, or dodgy background. Or he will be adopted once we have the Care Order by a new family who will put him first in all their decisions. He's so young we'll terminate any contact with his birth family when he's placed for adoption. What do you say to that?'

'Gosh, what a big step!' I said to Trish, my heart pounding, it all felt so important, such a huge responsibility.

'Well, in a way, the decision is all down to Kirsty, no-one else,' Trish explained carefully. 'If she's going to work with you, we have some foster carers who offer a mother and baby placement so Kirsty and Craig could be together and she would do the caring assisted by the foster carer until she's ready to do it all herself. Then we could look into putting her into her own home with Craig and other support so she can to learn to be independent.'

'Sounds good,' I replied.

'If on the other hand, if Kirsty doesn't work with you, or she only partly works with you, then we consider other family members. Craig's dad for instance. Otherwise I don't see that we have any choice other than to place him with adoptive parents for the rest of his childhood. What do you think to that?'

'Well,' I paused to think, it seemed so drastic and such a stark choice. But the more I thought about it the more I could see Trish was right. 'I think whoever has Craig needs to see his needs as a priority. And I need to make sure Kirsty knows how serious the situation is so that she can put all her effort into keeping him...'

'...if she wants to,' Trish interrupted me, her tone serious. 'I always used to really champion the parents to get them to look after their children and was so disappointed if that didn't happen. But after a while I came to see that sometimes people vote with their feet and just don't work with us, so no matter how hard I tried I couldn't place all children back with their parents. I don't want that to happen to you. Getting parent and child together will only work if they play their part.'

'Yes. I can see that,' I agreed. 'I won't take it personally if that doesn't happen'

'Good. What we really don't want is for anyone to agree to take him then not look after him properly. Whoever takes him has to make a real effort. OK?'

'Agreed,' I replied.

'Let the secretary know, won't you, so she can set up a child protection conference, ok?' She turned back to her desk and reached for the phone, a signal that she had work to get on with.

'Yes. Thanks Trish.' I went back to my desk.

Phew! Trish's words were a lot to take in and just so serious. But I had to agree that Craig's future was up to his mother, Kirsty. I would do all I could to help her access the help available, but if she didn't do her bit, then Craig would have to come first.

The Care Order transferred parental responsibility, that is all the duties of a parent, to the local authority, so we would make all decisions regarding Craig, until he was 18. Basically, that boiled down to me and my managers.

It seemed to me at first that child care social work was a huge round of meetings with different names and purposes so I decided to write them down in my diary, an ever growing font of information. 'Placement Planning Meeting - a meeting to agree the details of the placement, who the child can see when or where, who provides medical care etc. Case Conference - a meeting to decide whether to add a child's name to the register of children needing protection. Review - a meeting to discuss the arrangements made by the Placement Planning Meeting.' Phew!

Early in the 1950's history of child care legislation the law had been written with an underlying assumption that the state was always right. But when I started work in the late 70's some professionals had started to notice that the best outcomes for children were when the state worked *with* parents, helping those who were willing and able to care for their children to do so, not dictating to them. Before that, it was too readily assumed that single parents would be neither physically or morally able to look after their children so the children were often taken away, all contact barred, and new families found for them. This caused great distress to all parties.

Recently, local authorities had been using case conferences to make decisions about children who were mostly at home in worrying circumstances. The group of professionals working with the family, teachers, doctors, nurses, foster carers and most controversially, at first, the parents, would all be invited and the person chairing the meeting would ensure everyone had a turn to speak. A plan to ensure the child would be safe at home was the ultimate goal.

At first, many of the professionals didn't want parents to attend, citing the damage it could do to the relationship between the parent and the professional. But social workers insisted that if we were concerned enough about these children to arrange a case conference, then the parents needed not only to know, but to attend so they could challenge any concerns and learn how to change things to keep the child safe. And it worked. Case conferences, as most local authorities called them, became a cornerstone of the child protection system. They meant that the decisions about a child's future were shared around many people, which was much safer, especially for new social workers like myself who often got a barrage of assault from the media if things went wrong.

I rang Kirsty's Health Visitor to update her about the situation so they'd find Craig for his health checks and she could update his GP records. It would also be useful to have feedback from the surgery about Kirsty. I wanted to know about things like did she keep appointments for both her and Craig. That would tell us how committed Kirsty was to doing the best for both of them.

'I was worried about her and decided to visit her again if she hadn't been in to see me,' Health Visitor Sally Carpenter told me. 'Mother and baby were fine the first time I saw them when Craig was just a few days old. I suggested they come to clinic but didn't see them again so I popped in on my way home. It was quite a different story then. The baby was about six weeks old and unusually quiet. He had nappy rash and I gave him some cream and advice on how best to manage it. He was bottle fed but he hadn't seemed to have put on any weight. I thought Kirsty looked a bit down so I offered advice for the baby and about post natal depression and left Kirsty with details of the clinic so she could drop in. But she didn't turn up. I've been planning to see her since, but I haven't yet managed it. If things were the same, I would have referred the family to you then.'

I wished she had rung us at that point and checked out the GP records. Craig's GP, Nigella Smith, also rang back, but Kirsty had had no GP's appointments until late in her pregnancy. She didn't know much about mother and son either, they'd turned up for a couple of late ante-natal checks and had missed her post natal check so that didn't add a lot to the picture of Craig and Kirsty's life that I wanted to build up.

I made sure to keep some time free at 2pm so I could go and see Kirsty. Bob and Nancy had already agreed to meet me there. I needed to tell her that she would be entitled to have a free solicitor to advise her about the care proceedings and present her case at court if she wanted and talk about Craig's health. It was the solicitors job to advise her on the legal aspects of Craig's position and how to proceed to get the future she wanted.

I rang Janet to update her on Kirsty and to find out how Craig was. Apparently he'd slept fine and been no trouble. That worried me.

'Is he just a good baby or is he not used to being listened to by anyone?' I asked Janet, and we had to agree that we didn't know at that point.

Bob and Nancy were waiting for me outside the block of flats that Kirsty lived in. They had been waiting for me there too yesterday and gave me a friendly welcome on my arrival.

The area outside the flats was certainly busy. Young people were playing, dodging the cracks and craters of the tarmac, practicing bike tricks like hopping over a lump of concrete, playing football or going in and out of a garage with a broken door.

We walked upstairs to the flat and I rang the doorbell. I waited, almost willing someone to open the door. I had left a message saying to expect me. It would be much nicer to work with Kirsty and to have her co-operation. I wanted to help her overcome whatever was holding her back, if that was what was best for Craig.

I knocked on the door again and rung the bell. These things were running through my mind like a script as I waited. And waited. Bob and Nancy were next to me, Bob with his hands in his pockets shuffling about, Nancy with her arms wrapped round herself to ward off the chill. After a while Nancy shrugged her shoulders.

'I think they've thought of something better to do.' Bob joked.

'I suppose so,' I grudgingly agreed. Fortunately I'd already written a letter to Kirsty just in case, similar to the previous one. I popped it through the letter box, and thanked Bob and Nancy for their support. I made my way back to my desk and as I reached it, I heaved a big sigh of disappointment.

Becky noticed. She didn't miss much.

'Problems?' she asked, looking up from whatever she was writing. Multi-tasking was essential in this office to get through the workload.

'No-one in. I need to see Kirsty,' I answered trying to hide my disappointment. 'But I've put my contact details on another letter to her, so maybe she'll pop over.'

'You never know. One thing I have learnt is that clients can surprise you in ways you never expected.' Becky put her pen down and looked at me with concern.

'It is up to her isn't it?' I replied in low spirits. 'And I still don't know who Craig's father is or what happened to make him poorly.'

Becky put her phone down, crossed her arms in front of her and leaned towards me, helping to exclude some of the noisy hustle and bustle that was a permanent feature of our social work office. 'I used to get down too when I couldn't sort out other people's lives,' she explained. 'But I realised that every action a client makes, or doesn't make, is a statement, in a way. If Kirsty doesn't turn up or doesn't communicate at all, that tells you something doesn't it? It's the same as words, she just hasn't come out and said it yet. Of course it's always possible that there is some rational explanation. Maybe she's having some sort of emotional crisis and she isn't ready to speak yet?'

'That is perfectly possible,' I brightened up.

Becky looked at me with warmth. 'It could be that she's not ready to talk yet. It might be years before she's ready and you and Craig might have been off the scene for a long time before that. All you can do is get the world as right as possible for Craig.'

'I guess,' I replied. 'Perhaps I was hoping for too much.'

'That's the spirit,' Becky called as she returned to her writing. 'Write her a formal letter now, so she really knows how serious the situation is and what she can do about it. Suggest she sees a solicitor. It'll help if you send her a list of solicitors specialising in this type of work. Then she can take the letter to show them.'

'Great plan.' I brightened up a bit and got pen and paper.

Dear Kirsty, I am so sorry to have visited you twice in the last few days and found you not in. Craig is doing very well and you are welcome to see him by arrangement if you'd like.

We will need to consider Craig's future and I would like to include you in that decision. As part of the plans we will hold a Case Conference at a date yet to be arranged, and I'd be grateful if you could contact me to discuss this. My contact details are on this letter.

You may wish to use a solicitor to represent you in this and I enclose a list of local solicitors who deal with this area of work. This will be at no cost to yourself.

I look forward to speaking to you in the near future.

Yours sincerely, Carey Patterson,

Social Worker.

I thought about the tone, was it too formal? Or to chirpy and casual? I took it to Graham to ask since Becky was away from her desk. He decided it was fine, so I took it to the admin staff, who would type it out and give it to me one last time to sign it. Then off it went first class.

'I just took a call for you from the child protection meeting organiser,' Becky told me as I returned to my seat. 'She asked if you would call her back.'

'I'll do that straight away.' I called them and they told me the date they had set for the Case Conference for Craig. The admin staff had booked the room, contacted a senior manager to chair the meeting and sent out the invitations to everyone who was invited. It must have been quite a task.

I popped into Janet's on the way home and things were quite different there. I was welcomed in by Janet's husband Neil, who ushered me into the kitchen. I followed the warm, spicy aromas and found Janet preparing something that smelled really tasty for supper.

'That smells good,' I said as I took my coat off and sat on the chair Neil pulled out for me.

'Lentil dhal,' Janet said. 'Always popular in this house. Tea?' She held up a cup.

I nodded in thanks, I've never been known to turn down the offer of a cup of tea.

I could see Craig lying in a crib asleep at the side of the kitchen but I could barely recognise him he looked so different, even though he'd only been with the family a short while. His cheeks were more chubby, his skin brighter. I could see contentment in him as his little lips moved as if he was sucking, probably relishing the regular rhythm of warm milk, clean nappy, soft bed and sound sleep. It was hard to remember how he had appeared a week or so ago. He looked so different and that reassured me that I was right to move him.

Now I needed to do similar with Kirsty. Whatever happened in the future I wanted her to tell me exactly how those bruises got onto Craig and why he was so weak. I needed to keep an open mind as to what had gone wrong. Could she really have hurt Craig and been careless about his care? I wasn't sure.

'How is it going?' I asked, sipping my tea.

'Really well, I'm pleased to say.' Janet pushed a plate of home made biscuits towards me. She knew I'd never say no. I helped myself. She joined me with her own mug of tea. We walked towards Craig, who was just beginning to stir.

'Sally the health visitor came round earlier to weigh Craig. She confirmed he is underweight, so she gave me some advice on feeding and said she'd pop back next week.' We turned to look at him. His nappy rash is looking better now, isn't it, sausage?'

Craig was just waking up. He gave a sleepy yawn and stretched his arms and legs.

'Oh no! Have I woken you up?' I looked over at him. He looked impossibly tiny but totally gorgeous.

'He's just fine. It's time he woke up so hopefully he'll sleep better tonight.'

Janet picked him up and sat with him on her lap, next to me. He nuzzled his eyes with his fists before looking around him. I could see he was more relaxed now. It made a sharp contrast with the stress he had showed before.

'Has sleep been a problem?' I asked, picking up on Janet's comment. I knew Janet's husband and son worked and worried that they'd been woken in the night.

'No more than any other baby,' Janet reassured me. 'He does wake, it's not unusual for his age especially since he's underweight. But he is easy to feed and takes his bottle well. The rest of the family just sleep though any noise he makes.'

'That's good to hear.' I breathed a sigh of relief. 'I've still heard nothing from his mother, and we've still no idea who his father is.'

'What a shame,' Janet muttered. 'Poor little mite. Still, we're here when we're wanted aren't we?'

Craig will have had no idea what Janet was saying, but he looked up at her as if trying to focus on her face but with no other signs of recognition or a smile or anything. Perhaps he wasn't used to being spoken to. Kirsty had looked so depressed when I saw her it wouldn't have been surprising if that were the case.

'Would you like a cuddle?' she asked me.

'Yes, except that I wouldn't want to slow down his bonding with you,' I explained.

'He'll be fine. It's good to get him used to new people, especially since he will be moving on at some point.'

Janet passed him over to me. He felt so tiny and fragile. When I held him in the police station there was such a lot going on I didn't really have time to think about how he felt. I looked down and spoke to him in little baby chatter, but he didn't acknowledge me or any of the sounds I made. At least he didn't scream, I thought to myself.

'Should he be acknowledging others now?' I asked Janet.

'Possibly. But he hasn't had the best of starts so he might not follow the usual developmental patterns of other babies. I'm not worried about him. Yet.'

It was typical of Janet to be so tactful and was one of the things I liked about her.

I jiggled him about on my lap for a little while and told Janet about Kirsty, or rather Kirsty's absence and the child protection conference and she asked me about our plans which I explained before I handed Craig back and left.

People will always judge others and I know Kirsty hadn't shown herself in the best light in some people's minds. But it was so easy, especially at her young age, to get in such a muddle you don't know what to do for the best.

I could never judge anyone for what they did or didn't do and would try my best to help Kirsty, or anyone else in a similar position for that matter. I wanted to know what her mental health was like, was she depressed and was that mental state getting in the way of her bonding with Craig? I might need to have a specialist, psychiatric opinion on that. All those were things I was eager to help with.

But first I'd have to find Kirsty.

CHAPTER FIVE

I was fairly relaxed when it was time to go home, pleased that I'd got so much done. I'd worked late so I was alone as I went out to the car park. It was a cold and damp grey evening and I wasn't looking forward to the quick sprint to my car.

I was just searching in my pocket to get my keys when a woman's voice, shouted out, 'there!'

I turned to see where the sound was coming from and was taken aback to see a man, quite large, in a black hoodie running towards me and stopping just inches in front of me. The hood of his sweatshirt was pulled so far forward I couldn't see his features in the gloomy evening light.

'You,' he barked loudly in my face, pointing right at me, his fingers holding a cigarette and stopping just a little bit away from my nose.

'You 'ave upset 'er.' He pointed to a slim figure hunched up and standing at the top of a dark alley way nearby. I recognised the shape of her, the way she held her head, her shoulders slightly slumped, the slim silhouette. I knew who it was straight away - Kirsty and the guy she was with, probably Trevor. I glanced at him and turned to walk towards my car but my would be assailant darted ahead and blocked me, standing right in front of the car door so I couldn't open it. He seemed to take offence to the fact that I was ignoring him and giving him no eye contact whatsoever.

'D'you 'ear me?' He jabbed his finger towards me so close that I thought he was going to poke it right in my face. He stunk of booze and tobacco. 'She ain't done nuffin', nuffin, that she needs to be afraid of. D'you 'ear me?' He was really menacing. 'Or else you'll get this.' He shoved his fist up to my face. 'Right?'

I was frightened. Really frightened. Memories were going round in my head about Trevor's criminal record. I didn't know what to do but somehow I acted on autopilot. 'Excuse me,' I muttered, my hands shaking as I moved towards the car door.

Fortunately he did move aside and I put the key in the lock, but just as I was about to get in a thought came to me and I walked past the car towards Kirsty. My legs felt like jelly and I felt sick. With every step I took I worried that I was going to feel a fist come down on the back of my head or something like that. Yet my aggressor did or said nothing, he watched me incredulously and Kirsty just stared straight at me. As I approached she looked bewildered, disconcerted, embarrassed.

'Kirsty,' I said to her with all the courage of someone who hasn't thought this through. 'I've been to see you twice and left notes twice and got no reply. If you've got anything to say to me, please have the guts to come and say it to me in the office. I want to work with you, so that we both agree on what is the best way forward. But if you don't reply to my letters or speak to me, well I'm going to have to assume that you don't want to know and I'm going to have to do the planning by myself aren't I? Now that's where I work,' I pointed at the office. 'It says on both letters when it's open and there's a phone number. Come and see me and we can work something out.' And with that, I went back to my car.

My would-be assailant stood watching me, then swaggered off to join Kirsty and they both disappeared down the alley.

I got in the car but was shaking badly. It was one of those occasions when all the learning on the self protection courses my employers had sent me on should have kicked into gear and I should have just got myself out of that situation and said nothing.

But I had done the opposite.

I think what was driving me was worry. It's a big responsibility to have the future of a child in your hands and so far, other than taking Craig into care, I'd done nothing. Not for want of trying though. I knew my employers would insist on having this reported to the police, because the assailant might go on to harass other workers and the police would need to work out a pattern. It really wasn't on to frighten anyone like that, especially people who were trying to help you. But rather than go back to the office which I knew was empty anyway, I decided to go straight home and ring the police from there. I locked the doors of the car as fast as possible then willed the engine to come on immediately, which thank goodness it did.

As well as being scared, I was angry, especially at Trevor. How dare anyone speak to me like that? I realised that Kirsty was probably in a very low place, but the tone of my letters was always supportive and kind. Anyone so unreasonable as to frighten someone else like that really shouldn't be around children. Or fragile young women for that matter.

Never have I been so pleased to get home and shut the door behind me as I was that evening. 'I'm home!' I called and Fas, my husband, bought me a cup of tea in my favourite mug. I explained a summary of what had happened leaving out a lot because of confidentiality. I watched his expression change from cheerful and welcoming to concern as he saw the fear on my face and I told him a summary of what happened, leaving out names etc.

44

'You must to report that to the police,' he insisted. 'You need to be safe at work.' He was horrified, understandably.

I dialled the police's non-emergency number and explained what had happened.

'That's awful,' the officer taking my call agreed. 'The clients should speak to you somewhere you're safe, not threaten you when you're on your own. That doesn't solve any problems does it?'

I had to agree, and it was a relief to feel so supported.

I also rang our out of hours social work team. They manage emergency social care needs when the offices are shut, in case there were any repercussions that would involve them. We get to know the Out of Hours teams over time, they pop into our office for different things during the daytime and we pop into theirs when we handover cases. It was Rani who was on duty when I rang, we had had a brief social chat, he was in jovial mood when he heard my voice.

Then we moved on. 'I've got an incident that happened to me just now that I want to tell you about.'

He picked up immediately, probably from my tone of voice, that it was something unpleasant. 'What is it? Are you alright?' His chirpy tone had gone, replaced by tension.

'I was accosted by an angry client in the car park.' I went on to repeat the whole sorry tale.

'What a shameful thing to do!' I could hear the anger in Rani's voice. 'As if this job isn't hard enough without dealing with people like that. You're ok though?'

'Yes I'm fine,' I replied. I was fine now.

I reported the incident the next day in the office. 'I hope they find this young man and charge him, maybe with Kirsty as an accomplice. She is jointly liable,' Graham finished.

Kirsty probably was jointly liable I agreed, she was there and identified me. That wouldn't help her plan to look after Craig, if that's what she wanted. I couldn't stop a little voice in the back of my mind thinking this was her way of saying no, but I didn't dwell on that point.

What she'd done was dreadful, but I couldn't discount the fact that maybe there was some reason she did it. Perhaps she had mental health issues and her thinking was irrational, or maybe Trevor had bullied her into it. I knew at the moment I had to keep an open mind for Craig.

Later that morning as I returned from a visit Trish was looking out for me as I arrived. As I approached my desk she beckoned me over to her office, a small area partitioned off the main office space. Her expression wasn't her usual chirpy self, but deadly serious. 'Carey,

45

Inspector Jones tells me you were approached last night in the car park.' We all loved Trish, she cared, really cared, about her staff, you could hear it in her voice and instantly I felt soothed and cared for.

'Yes,' I replied, repeating the whole sorry tale. She listened, ignoring the busy office and concentrating solely on me.

'Are you sure you want to keep working on this case?' Tricia asked in such a way that if I had said no, she would have taken me off the task and not borne a grudge about it.

'Yes,' I reassured her. 'It was a shock, but I had expected this sort of thing would happen. My colleagues told me it is to be expected working in child protection. 'But Kirsty's role in this interests me and I want to find out more,' I explained. 'Maybe her relationship with Trevor was the driving force behind her lack of care for Craig? So maybe if Kirsty was single we could repair things between mother and baby?'

'That's a good point, Carey,' Trish replied. 'And it's worth asking these questions because if we do go ahead with the care order you'll need to give evidence in the witness box and will be grilled thoroughly by the client's solicitors to check that you have done everything to keep mother and child together.'

I gulped. 'I hadn't thought of that.'

Trish must have noticed the worry on my face. 'I've always found that if you've explored all the 'what if's and you absolutely knew your case inside out, you'll answer honestly, in detail and that will show you've done your job well. But Kirsty's solicitor will be expected to be thorough and challenging. The family will remember that day for ever and will need to know that their solicitor did everything possible to keep them together. So expect them to give you a hard time.'

'I see what you mean,' I said and went back to my desk. In social work you do have theories about a client's behaviour. They help you feel in control which is really helpful. But I hadn't thought that they would be useful for when I was cross questioned in court.

People were so kind to me in the office, listening as I recounted the tale yet again, whilst they made me cups of tea and gave me biscuits. This ritual was replayed every time someone had had a difficult time at work or with personal issues. It gave the team a lovely feeling of being like a family. It helped to take the stress out of every situation.

Later that morning two policemen who worked in the child protection team came into the office to see me. As usual, they didn't wear uniform just smart casuals. They were well known to us all so the receptionists just clicked the lock system and let them through. We are always ready with a cup of tea for visitors like police, occupational therapists, home carers and more. It made for a lovely way of doing work, you could talk about problems you might have with your clients over a coffee and the different perspective their training gave often suggested ways of resolving problems I'd never have thought of.

Jack and Kate were the two officers assigned to Craig and his mother. We sat back on the slightly more comfy chairs of the tea area with a few of my colleagues to chat all things child protection.

'Are you ok?' Jack asked. 'We were told about the car park incident. That must have been very frightening for you.'

'It was, I don't mind saying.'

'It must have been,' Kate sympathised. 'We've been to see Trevor and Kirsty. We left them in no doubt about how badly they've behaved towards you and told Kirsty to expect further action if there was another similar incident. We are considering further action against Trevor. They admitted that they'd had letters from you offering time to meet and had done nothing about them so there was absolutely no reason not to have seen you in the office.'

'Thanks,' I nodded. It felt good to be so well protected.

'We told them that if they have any queries, they must use the proper channels and contact you to discuss things. We don't think you should go alone to see them in future. Trevor in an angry mood is not a nice thing.'

'Thank you so much. I could do with visiting Kirsty to make sure she has the date of the Case Conference and about how Craig got those bruises and was so weak. He has been in care almost two weeks now. I don't feel particularly safe with them now. I wonder if their shouting at me was a prelude to something more violent. I'm very tempted to ask for a joint visit with yourselves.'

'Of course. A joint visit sounds like a good idea to me. I think in future you should ask them to come here to talk about things. We can't be sure you're safe with Trevor being so angry. How about going now? Have we got time?' Kate looked to Jack for confirmation.

Jack looked at his watch. 'Yes, we've got plenty of time.'

'Great,' I replied. 'There are a few things I need to speak to them about. I could get lots of queries answered in one visit.'

'Ok then. Off we go,' Kate said.

We finished our tea and using two cars as we were going different ways afterwards, met in the car park before going up the stairs to the flat. One hefty knock by Jack and the door was answered straight away by Trevor.

'Police and social worker,' Jack said as we held out our identity cards.

'Put that away!' Trevor growled at me looking at my identity card. 'I know who you are!'

'Can we have a word?' Kate asked.

Trevor looked at each of us with fury. 'Wot? Again?' he barked. He went indoors leaving the door open for us to follow him, which we did.

Kirsty was sitting on an armchair, huddled up and looking really despondent. She looked like she'd been crying, her face was puffy and her eyes red. She was looking down and fiddling with her long hair. Other than briefly checking us out, she give us no eye contact. She looked the epitome of depressed, just as she had on that fateful first day in the police station.

Trevor had a face like thunder. I could feel how difficult that could be for Kirsty to live with. He was a strong, stocky person with an air of intolerance about him.

'What d'you want?' he barked as he turned to sit in his chair.

'We're not here for you,' Kate answered briskly. 'So don't worry.

'This visit is primarily about Craig. So I need to speak to Kirsty.' I spoke only to Kirsty, as far as you could in a busy room. 'Is there somewhere we can go to speak privately?'

There was a gap till she answered, as if she wasn't sure what to say. Then she spoke. 'I…it's alright, tell me what you want here,' she said hesitantly.

'Even though it's not private?' I asked, my expression ensuring it showed I was happy to move if she wanted. 'I'm happy to move if you like? Just tell me where.'

'No. Talk now.' She didn't move from her position of being curled up like a baby, but she looked straight at me, lifting her gaze without lifting her head. At least I have eye contact I thought.

'Ok,' I replied. 'Well, there's nothing wrong with Craig, just in case you're wondering what the reason for this visit is. He's perfectly fine. It's because I've had such trouble finding you to speak to that I've come with Kate and Jack.'

'We've told Carey that you should go to see her in the office in future,' Jack stated baldly aiming his words at Trevor. 'It's not nice for her to be frightened like you did. And your record is not exactly a walk in the park is it?'

'Yeah, an' I'll tell you why an all,' Trevor barked in reply. 'None of them records as you call it, was my fault.'

'Enough Trevor,' Jack said sternly and turned towards Kirsty and I. 'We're here for something else now.'

'Whilst you're here,' Trevor got up and crossed the room, returning with a black plastic bag. 'You might as well take this with you.' He threw the bag at my feet. 'Take this to that lad of hers.'

It didn't sound good to me, 'what is it?' I glanced inside. Clothes. Baby clothes. 'Are they for Craig?'

'Yes. There's no point in having them here. They're only upsetting 'er,' he nodded briefly at Kirsty. 'She's done nothin' but cry the past few days. They just remind her of him. She needs to learn to get on without him now doesn't she? Now he's gone.'

I was horrified at what I was hearing and turned to Kirsty. She looked shocked and tears ran down her cheeks. 'Did you know about this?' I pointed at the bag.

'*No*,' she nodded tearfully.

I was furious, but I tamed down my anger, I didn't want to isolate Trevor too much until I knew how close to him Kirsty was. 'It is way, way too soon to decide that Craig won't be coming back to Kirsty.'

'But he's in care! It's obvious innit? You speak to Kirsty and see what she says about it,' he barked.

'I know he's in care, I know there are problems. But just because he's not here now doesn't mean we can't sort things out. It's way too early to plan the future for mother and son!' I was gritting my teeth, but had to be professional.

'Suit yourself.' Trevor gr'umbled. I was only trying' to be helpful.'

I turned away from him and spoke to Kirsty. 'First, we can arrange for you to see Craig at a contact centre if you like, second we need to discuss his future in private at some point, but there are things you need to think about first. If you wanted we could arrange for a mother and baby placement, so you could be with Craig and learn to look after him before moving on.'

'She don't need none o' your nonsense!' Trevor had a face like fury. 'Just make your mind up. Bring him back if that's what you're gonna do and she'll show you what she can do. Shouldn't 'ave been taken away in the first place and she don't need to go away now."

'Enough,' Kate held her hand palm outwards to Trevor and kept her attention on Kirsty.

Kirsty didn't answer my point about Craig. But I felt she had to know how serious the situation was, when people are low and depressed as Kirsty seemed to be, you can't be sure they're actually, really hearing what you say. 'Kirsty, we need to talk about Craig. Cos if we get a care order we'll look for an adoption placement. Tell me if that's what you want, but we've plenty of time to change that plan if you like,' I tried to be gentle, but also clear. Kirsty must be in no doubt that she has a choice.

There was no reply but I saw Kirsty's expression pale. It must have been difficult to hear that as Craig's mother I thought. But with a baby I knew that we needed a permanent, rock solid, family for him and sooner rather than later. Craig was getting older every day.

'I will keep offering supervised contact and a mother and baby placement because that is the way you could have him back - if you want to,' I explained with compassion.

'What do you think to that?' Kate asked Kirsty.

'That's up to her, innit?' Trevor growled moving his hefty body in the chair. 'Kirst wouldn't wanna be away from me in this fostering thing, would you babe?' He turned to her and asked.

Kirsty didn't reply. She did look thoughtful though.

'You don't need that placement thing, Kirst,' Trevor added.

I continued. 'Craig is young now but he needs a family. I can't make you change, only you can do that. But I can give you skills to help make caring for him easier if you like.'

'That's a fair offer,' Kate interjected. 'And one that you need to give some serious thought.'

'I do have one very important question to ask Kirsty.' I got my diary and pen ready to write the details down. 'Who is Craig's father as he needs to be informed?' I looked at Kirsty.

'Not guilty,' Trevor joked, laughing.

Kirsty didn't move and she said nothing, she simply shrugged her shoulders.

'Does that mean you don't know then?' I asked.

She nodded in agreement.

'Ok,' I nodded, planning to ask more details at some future date. Talking about Kirsty's ex might anger Trevor, and I didn't want Kirsty to have to deal with that.

One solitary tear ran down Kirsty's cheek. She brushed it aside with the sleeve of her sweatshirt. She had had a tough time romantically I guessed, and she'd know that Craig was doing well thanks to a complete stranger and not her. Those two things must hurt.

The only way I could support the local authority in taking this baby away from his mother was if she had been given every chance to change her mind. My words might have sounded harsh, brutal even, but Kirsty had to know without a shadow of doubt what the future held if she did nothing.

The room was silent for a moment. 'I have some things for you, important information.' I pulled out of my bag a letter with all our contact details, plus the conference details and the emergency duty service number on it. 'We have an important meeting that it would be good if you could attend. It's a child protection conference, it's about putting a child's name on a register, a bit like a warning system for all care staff. I can go through it with you in more detail if you like.'

'Craig don't need that,' Trevor interrupted. 'We've had enough of your sort puttin' yer nose in.'

'This is nothing to do with you,' Jack told him.

'We also have an out of hours emergency service but it is only for emergencies. If the query can be left till the office opens then that's what will happen.'

'Thanks.' Kirsty took the papers from me with tears in her eyes.

'Can I ask you Kirsty,' I asked, looking directly at her, 'if you have appointed a solicitor for the care proceedings?' It's never an easy topic to broach, but it had to be done.

Kirsty briefly looked over to us and whispered. 'No'.

'I have here another list of solicitors in town that are approved to take on child care work. I put a list in my last letter.' I passed the papers to Kirsty. 'There are quite a few to choose from. Don't feel you just have to take what I'm doing. You can challenge me in court if you like. It's getting the best for Craig that matters, and we have to make sure we are doing the right thing.'

Kirsty took the papers from me and glanced at them before putting them aside. I hoped that she would at least take an interest.

'Do come and see me in the office.' I had an inkling I wouldn't get more out of this meeting with Trevor in the background. 'Ring first if you can but if you're in the area you can just try if you like.'

'Well, I think we've done everything here, have you, Carey?' Kate asked looking at me. 'So long as you guys don't have any questions?'

Her gaze flicked from one to the other.

Trevor glanced at Kirsty, and then replied, 'no'.

'Ok, I'm ready.' I did up the zip on my handbag. 'Unless you have any questions for me? You've got the details about the conference, my contact details and details of solicitors for you.'

And with that, we left.

CHAPTER SIX

I was pleased that I had seen Kirsty and explained to her just how serious the situation was. All I could do now was get stuck into work. I had got some recording to catch up on, writing about each contact with a client, so I got stuck into that. Years into the future this would all be done on computer but this was well before office systems had been invented.

Anyway, the next day I was totally wrapped up in my work when Val from admin (administration - the office staff) rang to say someone was in reception to see me. I was puzzled and couldn't think who this could be.

To my surprise it was Kirsty. She was in the waiting room, looking lost and forlorn. My heart went out to her. I would say she looked sad, except that word simply doesn't sum up the vision I saw in front of me. Heartbroken, melancholy, devastated were more accurate. She looked paler than ever, her body tiny, thin, fragile, her legs wrapped up tightly together as if she wanted to take up the least possible amount of space in the world.

I felt for her and knew I would do my best for her, whether that was with or without Craig.

As I opened the door Val thrust a new box of tissues into my hand. 'I think you'll need these, poor lass,' she whispered. 'You're just the right person to speak to her. You're kind and understanding.'

I smiled at the compliment and took the box. Fortunately the interview rooms were all empty so I led her away from the busy pandemonium of the waiting room into a quiet little office. There were other mothers and babies in there, and that can't have been easy for Kirsty. She followed me meekly, making tiny steps as if she hadn't any right to be here and took a seat opposite me.

I didn't know how to open the conversation because I had no idea what she had come to say. It could have been to tell me she didn't want to cope with Craig and could I get him adopted or she'd like to learn to look after Craig and could I help her? So I opted for something neutral.

'Its nice to see you Kirsty,' and left it at that.

Kirsty gulped back some tears. It looked like she was struggling to get any words out. I passed her some tissues and waited for her response as she wiped her eyes.

'Are you ok?' I asked. I wanted her to set the tone. So I waited.

Kirsty fiddled with her tissue, pulling bits off and shredding it. It seemed like an age had passed till she answered and when she did it was just a nod - *yes*. Then she added to it.

'Can…can…I see Craig?'

I was delighted. I would have been ok had she asked me to get him adopted, but it is especially rewarding if you can help someone through a bad patch and set them up in a whole new life. It always worried me that if someone didn't fight to get their children back that they'd regret it later. But once a child is removed and adopted it's very rare to be able to revoke it, because the birth parent's rights are transferred to the adoptive parents.

'Yes, of course you can,' I replied. I knew there was one vital question I needed to ask her, although it was never easy. I said nothing about it at that point. 'If you wait here I'll make a few phone calls and see if we can go now, shall I?' Not all the interview rooms had a phone so I would have to go to the main office to use one.

Yes, she nodded again. I thought I could push a bit more whilst I had her here seemingly in compliant mode.

'Can I ask just one more thing?' I ventured before I left the room.

'Would you mind if we could stop at your doctors and asked them to see you? There might be some medication they can give you to help?' Depression is an awful thing, and I wanted to get Kirsty treated for it if necessary.

'No,' she replied baldly.

'That's a shame,' I tried to encourage her. 'It's very common to be depressed after just having had a baby. Do you feel depressed?'

'S'pose,' she swept her hair away from her eyes. 'Got a lot goin' on haven't I?'

'Yes. I know when people have got difficult things happening in their lives, they often think of harming themselves. Do you ever feel like that?' Brash as it was, I had to ask. The suicide rates are so high and I didn't want Kirsty to add to them even if that meant she would have to go to hospital.

'No…no…I'm alright, I won't do that,' she answered firmly.

'Ok then.' I looked at her wrists that were peeping out from under her jacket sleeve. They were thin and white. I was relieved there were no signs of self harm.

'I'll just ring and see about Craig. Back in a minute.'

I was disappointed that Kirsty wouldn't let me take her to a doctor. She had every reason to be depressed at the moment, I knew that, but I would like to have a medical opinion as to whether she needed medication or not.

There are times when you can force someone to see a doctor if they meet the criteria of the Mental Health Act, and I wanted to talk that over with a specialist. But I had spent some time on that in my training with them and I didn't see Kirsty as ill enough to warrant it. Her thinking was clear and rational even if she was making choices I didn't agree with. She didn't want to self harm so that was good.

I made my phone call and came back to the room Kirsty was in with my news. 'We're in luck! The foster carer is in town anyway and can take Craig to the Family Centre so we can go and see him there. The staff will look after him till we arrive. My car is just outside. Ready?' I asked pushing my arm through the sleeve of my coat. 'I can drop you wherever you want to go afterwards.'

'Ok,' Kirsty replied. I thought I detected a glimmer of a smile on her but I couldn't be sure.

The journey took about ten minutes so I thought it was a good time to ask questions that really needed answering. People are more relaxed in the car, perhaps because of the lack of eye contact and the fact that you have to stay where you are.

'Have you had any more thoughts about going to a specialist foster carer where you can go and stay with Craig?' I asked, hoping she'd thought it through. 'I can tell you more about the scheme if you like?'

'No,' Kirsty stated firmly.

'Ok,' I replied. There was another question I needed an answer to, so I asked it. 'I'm sorry to be so intrusive, but it really matters. Who is Craig's dad?'

'I dunno.' She replied after a pause, in a curt manner.

'Ok. Can you tell me what you do know about him? Because he does have parental responsibility and we need to include him in our future plans.'

'I dunno,' she replied casually. 'I slept with a couple of different blokes, then I never saw them again. And no, I don't know where they are now or even their names.'

'You didn't even know their names?' I screwed up my face in confusion. 'Surely you must've known what they were called?'

She shrugged her shoulders. 'It's not that weird. I was at a festival. One bloke was called Woody, and the other was called Red Dog. Dunno why.'

'Would you even know the person that introduced you? Wouldn't they know how to contact them?' I threw out any idea I could think of that might lead me to the missing father.

'There wasn't no person that introduced us. I was queueing up to get a drink and this guy talked to me. He was alright so we spent the night together. Same the next night, different bloke. It's not illegal is it?' Kirsty spoke in a challenging way, as if defying me to criticise.

'Suppose not. I just haven't heard that sort of thing before. Thanks for telling me though.'

Kirsty shrugged her shoulders in reply.

'What about other relatives? Do you have parents or brothers or sisters?'

'Dunno where they are. I don't have nuffin' to do with my family these days.'

We pulled up outside a modern single storey building its windows covered with jolly posters and children's artwork in beautiful bright colours. 'This is it,' I explained to Kirsty. Her skin paled and her body posture froze briefly. But she followed me out. I pressed the buttons to enter and the door clicked open.

One of the staff walked towards us, snuggling a little baby to her. Craig.

'Hi, I'm Hazel,' she said, 'and here is Craig. He's just been fed and changed,'

He was beautifully clean. He was lying in Hazel's arms, quite contented. I thought it must be hard for Kirsty to see him being held by someone else. We went inside.

'He's in different clothes,' Kirsty looked straight at him.

'Yes,' I replied. 'Do you want to hold him?'

Kirsty didn't reply but stepped forwards so Hazel could pass him to her. It was my job to notice how she was with Craig and how he reacted to his mum. I needed to put that in the report I would write for court. I tried to watch without judgement.

Kirsty looked a bit awkward, as if she wasn't used to holding babies. I guessed she'd forgotten, it had been three weeks that he'd been in foster care. Kirsty's arms weren't in the right place at first and she didn't support him properly behind his back. Hazel lifted Kirsty's arm up to a more helpful angle as she passed the child to his mother. All these things could be shown to her if she chose to go to the mother and baby placement I'd suggested.

I leaned forward and made cooing noises to Craig, holding his little fingers in mine briefly as much to show I approved of his mother holding him than anything else.

'There's a room free over here,' Hazel pointed to the door. 'We'll bring you coffee. You'll need to sit down, your arms will ache soon. He's heavy.'

As babies go, he didn't look very heavy, but big enough to make anyone's arms ache if held him for any length of time. Kirsty and I went into the room, found some seats and were bought warm drinks.

'How does it feel being with him now?' I asked.

'Alright,' she replied, in a tone which was difficult to interpret. I watched her body language which I'd be expected to write up for our records. She hadn't relaxed into a motherly pose yet, perhaps because she was out of practice as Craig had been away from her. She didn't hold Craig particularly close, making it difficult for him to to snuggle up to her. I tried not to criticise even in my mind, just watched in a supportive, caring way.

She jiggled him around on her lap and spoke to him gently, it was really sweet but Craig became fidgety and restless. I felt for her. 'Babies never do what you want them to, do they?' I sympathised. It had probably taken a lot for her to come and see me and with Craig being restless it had probably upset her.

A few minutes later Kirsty began to glance out of the window. I was disappointed that she didn't give Craig her full concentration. At first I wondered if she was waiting for a lift home from someone else, but then I realised she couldn't have been. I said I'd give her a lift anywhere and this wasn't a long standing arrangement.

That was odd, I thought. As she hadn't seen Craig since he came into care and had asked to see him, I expected her to be unable to take her eyes off him.

But that didn't happen.

Craig began to wiggle and fidget.

'Would you like to try changing his nappy now, in case that's what's making him fidgety?' I asked Kirsty. 'There are fresh nappies here I'm sure.'

'N..n..no,' she said, passing him to me. 'I gotta go.'

'Oh, why? Don't you want a lift?' I held my hands out to receive the baby, but was puzzled. 'You can spend more time with Craig if you like?'

But she didn't answer and seemed rushed, as if she simply didn't want to be here anymore.

'You change him,' she said. Once he was with me Kirsty dashed across the room without a second glance. Hazel must have wondered what was going on and came towards us, but Kirsty just ran past her and out of the room door. A few moments later I heard the main door slam and watched her cross the road, still in a hurried way and without looking back.

I hadn't learnt much from what she said, other than the brief conversation about Craig's father.

But I wouldn't let my expectations get in the way of judging Kirsty. It could be that she was depressed, it needn't be that she didn't want to see Craig. I mustn't let myself forget the fact that Kirsty could change all that if she wanted.

But her reaction to holding him today worried me. It wasn't the end of the road yet, but earlier that afternoon I thought I'd had a breakthrough, but now things didn't look so promising.

CHAPTER SEVEN

'It's a very serious situation. The legal department want answers and they want them now,' Graham explained to Nitin, a senior manager from a different office who had come in as an independent person to chair the child protection meeting.

Graham's brow was furrowed with tension. 'We have secured Interim Care Orders. They only last a month so they have to keep being renewed. We're constantly being reminded of that by the legal team. We need to make long term plans for Craig. The court need to know what we are doing. If we take a child into care it's not like a hotel stay, we need plans for this child's future, we need to do something now.'

'I'll do my best Graham,' replied Nitin, looking equally stressed. 'I will ask everyone at the conference about Craig's father, just in case anyone has more detail about him. Other than that I don't know what else we can do.'

'Me neither,' Graham ran his fingers through his hair. 'I can quite see legal's point. Two people make a baby, and not finding Craig's dad deprives that person of his child.'

'I know. But all I can do is add it to the agenda and ask everyone,' Nitin agreed. 'But if Kirsty doesn't know, there's not a lot more we can do.'

'Quite. Thank you anyway for doing your best,' Graham touched his hand on Nitin's shoulder as they both left the office and headed in the direction of the meeting room.

Almost every body working with Craig was at the Child Protection Conference. As well as the chair to chair the meeting and somebody to take the minutes there were both my managers Trish and Graham, Jack from the police child protection team, Sally the health visitor and Maya from fostering and adoption who would represent Janet. We didn't want Janet to come. Kirsty was allowed to bring support and that might well be Trevor, and if either recognised Janet or found out where she lived it could put her and her family at risk. But both myself and the person from the fostering and adoption team had asked Janet and her family her thoughts so we could include them in our decision making. All the decisions about children in care were for the local authority to make. Although they would consult everyone, it was they that had parental responsibility.

Of course Nitin's assistant was there to take the minutes and distribute them to all attendees and Kirsty afterwards. The only person who wasn't there and had only sent a report was Dr Gladstone. This was typical of doctors. They usually only saw themselves as part of identifying the problem, not in addressing the solution so they rarely attended.

The person we really needed there was Kirsty. I had tried to share my report with her earlier in the week but she hadn't been in when I called, even though I left a note giving the time I'd visit and a copy of the document. It would have been great to have heard her views in person, so we could include them in our future planning. But I guess it was no surprise to me that she wasn't here. She wasn't engaging with me or anyone else on Craig's care team at all other than that one brief afternoon visit.

When we were all in the meeting room ready to start we waited five minutes after the planned start time in case she turned up. But no such luck so we introduced ourselves for the benefit of new staff and carried on.

'It seems that Kirsty isn't coming and we need to start because the room is booked when we've finished,' Nitin began. 'Sadly Kirsty has chosen not to join us. But you will all have had a copy of Carey's report and I trust you've read it so we all know why Craig is in care and don't need to go back to the beginning again. Caz, could you start by telling us what you've been doing with the family?'

'There's not much to say really. I have had a lot of difficulty contacting Kirsty. I don't get an answer when I knock at her door although she did come to see me here once and we went to see Craig at the Family Centre. But that didn't go well. Kirsty left quickly despite the fact that I had offered to drop her wherever she wanted afterwards and wasn't trying to hurry her up. She just walked out of her own accord early, without explaining why. I'm at a loss to know what the problem was. On a good note though, Craig is happy with Janet, but we do need to plan for his future, I know that.'

'Hmm. That doesn't look good for Kirsty's ability to parent does it?' Nitin reflected. 'Let's hear from Sally the Health Visitor.'

'I had similar difficulties to yours when I visited the family at their home,' Sally began. 'Kirsty's never in or if she is she doesn't answer the door. She didn't bring Craig to clinic during the few weeks she had him. But I did have some news this morning. I had an update from Dr Miriam Gladstone.' She waved a letter in the air. 'It's detailing Craig's health since coming into care. She says he's doing well, he is gaining weight and his nappy rash has gone. But she's unsure yet whether he has any underlying conditions, she says his cognitive skills are still behind, which may be attributable to his life so far, so she'll keep him under review.'

'Thank you,' Nitin looked around at the group. 'And the Police? Do you have anything to add?'

'Just that we've charged Trevor with harassment since they accosted you in the car park, Caz. I think Kirsty will just get a caution, she was quite clear Trevor was the guiding force in that episode and he didn't dispute that,' Jack explained. 'We're having trouble charging either of them with assault following the bruises on Craig, because it's not clear who is responsible, it could even be a third party. We haven't given up on it yet though.'

'Thank you for that feedback Jack. Now, Graham, I know you need to discuss something, would you like to continue?' Nitin looked in Graham's direction.

'Thank you. Legal department say we need to do more to find Craig's father, especially if the child doesn't go back to his mother.'

'If we get a care order and he is adopted,' Trish explained for those who might not know, 'that would take his father's parental responsibility away, and that isn't fair on either Craig or his dad.'

'But Carey's had no success finding out anything from Kirsty about him,' Graham continued making his point. 'That means we'll have to advertise in both local and national papers for either the fathers or anybody who might have any interest in or information on a baby born on Craig's birthday, using the nicknames we have for his possible fathers and hopefully that might bring somebody in who can tell us more. I can't see what else we can do, but if any of you know anything we would be grateful to hear about it.'

'I found the same thing,' the Health Visitor said. 'I first met Kirsty when she'd just got out of hospital, she wouldn't tell me anything about Craig's father other than to say it was down to one of two quick flings she had at a festival. She didn't even know the men's proper names, they were just known by nicknames.'

Jack from the Child Protection Police spoke up. 'I spoke to DS Sheila Murray, she knows a lot about the people who live in that area. She believes this is true since Kirsty was single last summer until she hooked up with Trevor.'

'Thank you for that,' Trish replied. 'Can you all stay vigilant in all your dealings with the Kirsty and try to find out more information? Ideally we want to include Craig's father in any plans. We don't want to isolate him.'

'We might not have any choice if we can't find him,' I piped up.

'I am quite clear that we are planning either to get Craig adopted or for his mother to have care of him if she will take advantage of our offer of a mother and baby placement to learn to care for him - properly this time,' Trish stated.

'Obviously with a child as young as Craig he needs to be with a family he can build lifelong bonds with,' Graham explained. 'If Kirsty proves she's committed to Craig, we'll give her all the help she needs. But we're not having a 'will I won't I' situation that goes on for months. Craig needs a family of his own and he needs it fast. If Kirsty doesn't put all her energy into him and we can't find dad, we'll find an adoptive family for him. There is no alternative. I'll let the legal team know this is our plan. It is a time of waiting, I understand the concern. But we do have plans and we won't wait long until we know which of them we'll act on, after all, the court isn't ready to hear our final application yet, there's always a delay in the court from when we apply to the actual hearing.'

'I'm pleased to hear steps forward are being made,' stated the Health Visitor. 'This child needs to be settled as soon as possible.'

'That sounds like a reasonable way forward. Legal department just wanted to know what Craig's future was.' Nitin summarised the decision, looking around the room. 'In terms of the purpose of this meeting, whether we should include Craig's name on our Child Protection Register in the categories of neglect and physical abuse, because his future is not yet clear, I'm guessing we'll all say yes.'

He asked each person for their response and they all agreed.

'Right. I think we're done now. Craig will be put on the child protection register in the categories of neglect and physical abuse,' Nitin snapped his diary shut. 'We'll be back here to review the situation I propose in around two months, depending on when the admin. staff are able to book the room.'

He drew the meeting to a close.

Now the meeting had finished I had to tell Kirsty the result. I didn't just want to say 'Craig is now on the child protection register in the categories of physical abuse and neglect,' because that would be so demoralising for her in the position she was in and could totally wreck any chance of reuniting mother and son.

Even though that was looking unlikely, her being in the position she is, with an abusive partner, no job, no helpful family, that must be soul destroying. Giving that sort of message would surely completely crumple her.

To give her the best chance of being Craig's mum, I had to support her and build her up in order to help her turn her life around. I knew the time would come, and not so far off, that I would have to make a decision and cut Kirsty out of Craig's life if nothing had changed in her commitment to her son. But that time was not yet. There was time still for me to help Kirsty without it impacting negatively on Craig. I wrote her a letter.

'Dear Kirsty, as you might remember we had a child protection conference here today concerning Craig. You will get the minutes from the Chair of the conference in due course, but I would like to discuss the result with you and would be grateful if you could contact me. I'd also like to discuss setting up some regular contact for you and Craig if you'd like. Please let me know when you're available.

Many thanks, Carey Patterson.'

I couldn't change the fact that Kirsty would get the details of the conference from the conference team, but I could change how she responded to them. I got an envelope for the letter, stuck it down and dropped it in the 'Post Out' tray.

I had begun to give up on the idea that Kirsty might drop in and see me again and reconciled myself to the fact that, for whatever reason, she either didn't want to or wasn't able to, care for Craig. It looked like I would be keeping him in care and looking for an adoptive family for him when the court had made the care order. But then I had a glimmer of hope.

I was just sitting at my desk about to leave early to go to an appointment when the phone on my desk rang. It was Val, the receptionist.

'Carey, is that you? I've got someone to see you in reception.'

'Oh, who is it?' I asked.

'It's that young woman who came to see you a few weeks ago, the one I gave you the tissues for - but, you'd better be prepared.'

'That'll be Kirsty. What do you mean Val, when you say be prepared?' I asked, puzzled.

'Well...' she answered. 'She's not...well, she looks like she's had a hard time, let's just leave it at that.'

'Ok,' I mumbled, none the wiser.

I could see Kirsty in the waiting room looking down at her shoes, as I walked past reception. I couldn't really see her face but her body was all hunched up in her usual depressed pose.

I went into the waiting room. 'Hello.' I said, but Kirsty didn't move a muscle, her head was still down. I wondered if she was hiding something. 'There's a small room free, shall we go in there?'

Kirsty lifted her head slowly, then Val's comments fell into place. I took a deep breath and tried to hide my shock. She got up and followed me into the room where we sat at two chairs on the same side of a desk. I could see her properly now. One eye had a dark purple bruise and there were various smaller bruises and little cuts spread about her face. She noticed me looking at it and lifted her hand to touch them, but her hand shook so badly she couldn't control where it went and she put it back on her lap.

'I know what you think it is,' Kirsty's voice was faltering and weak, 'but I...I... fell down the stairs.'

I didn't believe her for one minute and ignored her excuse. 'Kirsty that looks painful. Did Trevor do it?'

'No, no...' she shouted and burst into tears.

'If you had fallen your bruises would be on the side of your face that you landed on. Those are all over the front of your face. It was Trevor wasn't it?'

There was no answer, just sobs, sobs that wracked her whole body. I passed her some tissues. Her silence confirmed my view.

'I hate anyone who treats others like that.' I spoke quietly and calmly. 'Hitting others should not be allowed. It isn't allowed. Have you been to the police?'

There was a long silence. I waited sympathetically.

'It was my fault,' she choked out between sobs. 'I annoyed him.'

'That does not make it your fault,' I stated plainly. 'People disagree all the time whether they live together or not. You don't beat people up just because they disagree with you.'

A new bout of sobbing took over, and long, haunting, fearful sighs.

'Let's get you out of there and into a refuge now. Today,' I offered, picking up the phone to make the arrangements.

She put her hand on the receiver. 'No, no. I need to talk to him.'

'No you don't. I can do that or the police.' I held the phone in the air. 'I'll ring the refuge now to arrange a place for you, then I'll go round with the police to Trevor's place, collect your things and tell him that you won't be back.'

'He'll come and find me.' Kirsty sobbed. 'I know it.'

'No-one knows where the refuges are, the addresses are secret. And if he does find you, the people who are in charge of the front door are very skilled. They know exactly how to deal with angry people. And at the first sign of trouble they ring the police. No-one gets through there, you will be safe.'

'I...I...can't. Trev's a great guy, he's just misunderstood. He'll be so sorry for what he's done when I see him.'

'Kirsty no-one should be treated like you have been. You can run miles from him, and you'll have our help and support. And if you are serious about having Craig back there's no way we can do that whilst Trevor is on the scene.'

For a moment Kirsty stopped sobbing and listened intently. I put the phone down and spoke. 'The only way I can see we'd let you have Craig back is if you'd properly split up from Trevor, spent a while in the refuge getting yourself together then moved onto a mother and baby foster placement. That will mean the foster carer looks after both of you, and teaches you how to look after Craig until you're able to look after both of you yourself.'

'So what you're saying is it's either Trevor or Craig?' Kirsty looked at me wide eyed.

'No-one would put any child anywhere near a violent man like that. We can stop Craig being anywhere near him, but sadly I can't stop you. So yes, I guess that is what I'm saying. Trevor or Craig.'
Little did I know that in the next twenty years or so's time the police would have powers to apprehend an abuser without the victim's approval.

But that was in the future.

'What I had hoped to do today was to set up regular contact between you and Craig and increase that if it went well and you were able to keep up regular visits. But the evidence against Trevor is now so compelling we wouldn't want Craig to have anything to do with him.'

'Oh,' she muttered.

'Now, let me set up that refuge.' I picked up the phone again.

'No! No!' Kirsty shrieked, put her hand on the receiver and ran towards the door, opened it and was about to go through.

'Think about what I've said,' I asked as she was leaving. 'You're too nice to allow yourself to be treated like that.' I don't know if she'd heard or not, she'd gone before I'd even finished my sentence.

A chill went down my spine, I knew what I would have to do. If Kirsty didn't turn her life around in the next few weeks, I would have to take this child away from her for the rest of his childhood. We physically had Craig and pretty soon we'd ask the court to take Parental

Responsibility away from Kirsty and Craig's dad, if we ever found out who he was. I didn't have a problem with that. But I had to give Kirsty every chance to change. I could see there was a wonderful person beneath all that muddle and sadness and I'd love to see her reunited with her son.

Craig was young now and research showed he'd settle quickly with a new family. I couldn't allow Kirsty's confusion to lead to an extended period of uncertainty. Craig deserved better than that.

Now, it was over to Kirsty.

CHAPTER EIGHT

About ten days passed before I heard from Kirsty again. In that time the legal department had placed adverts in local and national papers asking for information from anyone who might know something about Craig's father. I'd been to see Craig who was getting on well and written the first part of the report I would have to produce to the Family Court when it was time for the final hearing.

I was completely engrossed in getting the paperwork ready for another client when Val from reception rang to tell me I had another visitor.

'It's your lady with the bruises,' she said. 'She doesn't look any better than she did last time, bless her!'

'Aw, I'm doing my best, honest,' I replied, hoping for some changes in Kirsty.

I saw her through the windows in reception as I passed. Last week's bruises were fading but I thought I saw some new ones. She had a big bag with her, I hoped that was a good sign. I clicked through the doors and we went into a little side room to talk privately. I greeted her with warmth.

'You look like you've been through the wars again,' I sympathised, I could clearly see more bruises now.

'Yeah.' She spoke timidly and nodded.

'Trevor again?'

'Yeah.' Loud sobs racked through her. 'I can't go back there.'

I couldn't help a little thrill going through my heart, this is just what I wanted to hear. 'When did you decide that?'

'A few days ago. We had an argument and...' she pointed to some bruises on her forehead. 'He said sorry and all that and was nice for a while. But I knew this is how it's going to be for ever. He's always gonna hit me even if he does say sorry and he'll never do it again. And then I thought even if I did get Craig back it would be bad for him too.'

'It would,' I agreed.

'Trev wants me to leave Craig with you and have more babies of our own. But I don't want to have babies with him. No way.'

'If you did stay with Trevor and have more babies you run the risk of them being taken into care too. No social worker will want a child to live with a violent person, man or woman if they're not totally sure the mum will protect them. It's just too dangerous.'

I watched her grimace at the thought, but let her ask me about plans for the future.

'Is it still alright to go to that place that you said?'

'The refuge? I think so. I'll just ring and check.'

One phone call later her place was secured.

'Can I see Craig?'

'Yes, in time, just let's get you sorted first. Have you got many things at Trevor's? Does he know you're not coming back?'

She nodded. 'I shouted that I wasn't coming back as I left, but I couldn't carry everything so I gotta go back.'

'No. I can do that. I'll ask the police to come with me.'

'Can I come too?' She looked straight at me, a tiny gleam of pleasure in her eyes.

I hadn't thought of her going, I guessed she'd want to stay away. This was a side to her I'd never seen before. I was delighted.

A few more phone calls and a car ride later and we were at her flat. I'd asked for a police escort and we had two constables with us I'd never met before. They seemed nice though.

Kirsty used her key to get in, the police and I followed her.

Trevor was sitting on the sofa watching the racing on TV, with a can of beer on a coffee table and a cigarette balanced on the edge of an overflowing ashtray in front of him. The whole room stunk of cigarette smoke, a thick fog of the stuff was hanging around the room at shoulder height.

'What you doin' here? And what the fuck are they doing here Kirst?' He sneered in our direction. 'Tell me wot's goin' on babe?'

I saw his eyes well up with tears. I thought he was going to tug Kirsty's heart strings with some emotional plea or another. I willed Kirsty to ignore him.

'Kirsty's getting her stuff, and we don't want any trouble do we?' a burly police officer replied, standing above Trevor with his arms crossed and a don't mess with me expression on his face.

Kirsty went around the different rooms grabbing her things and I stood behind her holding bags open for her to throw things into.

'These two are here to make sure you don't hurt me again,' Kirsty said as she chucked some mens underwear in Trevor's direction. It hit him right on the nose. 'You've treated me like shit! I'm moving out and not coming back!'

'Who says?' Trevor looked around himself, sneering and pulling faces. 'I've told you love, you'll never cope on your own. You haven't got it in you. How many times have we been over this? Cor, I must have the patience of a saint to put up with you. Look, you tell these buggers to clear off and you can stay, and we'll say no more about it. How about that love?'

'She said no,' I replied, struggling to stay professional. I really wanted to give him a mouthful myself, but best not, I realised.

It seemed the policeman felt the same too.

The constable got closer to Trevor and hovered over him, invading his body space in a way that could almost be menacing. 'She doesn't need your advice,' the officer growled. 'You should be ashamed of yourself.'

At least Trevor did have the decency to look away.

'My colleagues will be wanting to have a word with you. So I shouldn't go too far.' The officer looked down at Trevor.

'All right mate! I get it!' Trevor put his hands up in the air palms out, and sat as meekly as a mouse, I would go so far as to say he looked intimidated.

I must admit, I may not have challenged him in the same way because I didn't have the physique, but I couldn't disagree with anything the policeman said or the way he said it. Quite the opposite. I was pleased someone had been gruff with Trevor.

I watched Kirsty busily gathering things. She looked different somehow, I couldn't quite work out in what way but then I realised, she held her head higher than I had ever seen her do before, her chin just a little bit raised. Good on you girl, I thought.

It's so easy to get yourself in a mess, especially when you're young or a bit overwhelmed in life, but it is hard to pick yourself up when you're low. Kirsty had taken the first step and I was proud of her.

'Right, I'm done.' Kirsty had four big bags stuffed with clothing.

'I'll help with that, the policeman said grabbing two. I took one whilst Kirsty took the other.

'We'll be going then,' I said, and turned towards the door letting Kirsty go first just in case Trevor had any ideas.

'Oh Kirst…' Trevor shouted. 'Keep in touch.'

'Fuck off,' she replied, without a backward glance.

That's the girl, I thought as we were coming downstairs.

The policemen helped us load the car and went on their way.

'Thank you,' Kirsty said

I was proud of her and it boded well for her future. But I knew only too well it was early days yet. Many abused people give into temptation and try again with their violent past lovers, spurred on no doubt by slick talking, gifts and promises. It was a spiral I could see was difficult to escape so I mustn't be tempted to allow too much contact between

Kirsty and Craig. I didn't want him to get too attached to her only for her to go back to Trevor. Only time would tell if she could stick with it.

'Ok then, we'll go straight to the refuge now.' Kirsty stood by the passenger door as if uncertain whether to get in or not. 'The door's opened for you.' I invited her and she got in slowly.

It was quite a long drive from Trevor's house. Luckily there was only one room available and it was at a refuge quite a distance away. I thought that worked out quite well because I didn't want her to bump into Trevor whilst shopping and most refuges won't take people living close to them because it puts them at greater risk of their ex finding them. The only downside was that it would make it harder for her to keep in touch with friends, if she had any, but there was a bus service.

We had a long talk in the car. I was curious as to what Kirsty's mood would be. Happy? Concerned? Tearful? Wary? Or probably a bit of everything.

She was quiet so I chatted away telling her what I knew about the place, hoping that a bit of knowledge would help her feel at home quickly. 'It's run by a lady called Kurian, I've met her at training events but not actually been to the refuge. She is very kind, you get a great feeling of warmth when you speak to her. She's had a hard time herself fleeing a war in her country, so she really understands how tough life can be.'

Kirsty listened attentively.

'The address is secret so don't give it to anyone else. Even with all the precautions there are a few ex's who have found it so they do get some trouble sometimes. But the security there is very strict and police come round straight away at the first sign of trouble. The staff are very skilled at coping with these events.'

I glanced over at Kirsty. It was impossible to tell what was going through her mind by her facial expression. I wondered if I'd gone overboard by telling her too many negative things so I changed tack.

'People tell me what a feeling of relief they get when they enter a refuge. There are quite a lot of other staff and volunteers as well as Kurian and of course many people who have been through the same thing you have. But everyone is kind and understanding. Some of the staff have had violent partners themselves, some have had a hard time for other reasons and some just care.'

'Do all the people that live there have kids?' Kirsty asked.

'It varies. Some do, some don't. Does it matter?'

'S'pose not'

'D'you like kids?' I asked.

'Yeah.'

'Did you have brothers and sisters to play with when you were young?'

'No.' There was silence.

'Were you an only child?'

'Yeah. It was just me and mum. But she was out a lot anyway, at work and things.'

'So who babysat you?' Kirsty looked forlorn, lost even.

'For a while there was one of my mum's mates next door. I'd go round hers, then she'd put me to bed in my room in mum's house and I could bang on the wall if I wanted anything.'

'So no one was with you in the house?' I asked, my toes curling up in horror at the 'parenting' Kirsty seemed to have had.

'No. Just me. It was a flat not a house, in a big block of flats.'

No wonder Kirsty had struggled caring for a baby alone. I felt so sad for her. She'd had a dreadful role model. 'So how long for? When did your mum get back?'

'Mum worked in a couple of pubs so it would be after closing. They usually had lock ins for the regulars so it was often very late.'

'Weren't you frightened?' I asked in horror.

'I didn't know no different,' came the blunt reply.

'Have you got any other relatives, grandparents? Aunts? Uncles?'

'Dunno. I think mum had a couple of sisters and a nan. But I never seen them.'

'What an awful start you've had in life, being left alone in a flat to go to sleep. That wouldn't be good enough today,' I explained. 'I can only think the authorities didn't find out about it, it's clearly neglect.'

Kirsty shrugged her shoulders.

'It wasn't your fault though,' I reassured her. 'Do you see much of your mum now?' I asked. I know she had been asked this before but I wanted to make sure I had the right grasp of Kirsty's family so I asked again.

'Nope,' came the abrupt reply. 'Haven't seen her for a couple of years. Dunno where she is even. She went to live with some bloke. We never got on so I stayed for a while with a couple of my mates, then I got a room when someone moved out of my mates house. I was there for a few months maybe, then I went to stay with Trev.'

'Oh I see,' my heart was aching for her. How difficult her life was. I felt privileged to be able to help her.

No answer.

'You've had a very difficult start in life haven't you?'

'I don't know if my life is difficult,' she explained. 'I got nothing to compare it with have I?'

'S'pose not,' I agreed.

I looked around at her, not willing to say what I was going to say next unless I was sure it wasn't going to upset her more. Her life is in transition at the moment and I didn't want to give her more problems to think about. But she still had the confidence I'd seen as she left Trevor, so I went for it. It can be quite liberating to know you're not the only person suffering the same feelings. 'I think you've got an attachment disorder you know.'

'What's that?' She looked puzzled.

'Because you were so young and didn't find it easy to look after yourself you latched onto someone who seemed to offer love and support. And if that didn't work out you found someone else to try to do the same thing. Trevor.'

Kirsty looked really engaged with this conversation, she wanted to know the details. 'So is that like a mental health thing?'

'No, not really. You've had a difficult childhood with a mum who had maybe had the same sort of childhood herself, so you never learned to look after yourself from your mum because she couldn't teach you. It's a bit like if your parents never taught you to ride a bike you have to learn to ride a bike later. Only its not bikes for you its looking after babies.'

I looked round at her when road traffic conditions allowed. She was thinking, really thinking. 'So it wasn't my fault then all this stuff with Craig and Trev?'

'No. You were looking for someone to show you how to care for a baby and yourself, and because you have low self esteem and didn't know what to look for in a partner, you chose the wrong person?'

'So it's not really my fault then?' I could hear a brighter tone in her voice.

'No.'

'It's me mam's fault then?'

'Well, maybe. I don't know what her childhood was like and maybe she didn't have the right sort of teaching either. These things can go down the generations, so I wouldn't want to blame her. You can change the pattern though.'

'It kind of adds up. So how do I change it? Just pick better blokes?'

'Sort of. It's about giving you different skills. I'm hoping we can teach you about proper parenting at one of our mother and baby placements if you want to bring Craig up. A foster mum can be like a mum to you too, and show you what to do.'

'So I'd stay in someone else's house?'

'Yes, with Craig. You'd have your own room for both of you. Caring for Craig is down to you, but you get help, especially in the early days.'

She didn't answer for a while. So I prompted her. 'That should give you better self esteem, so you won't be so tempted to choose a partner who can't look after you properly. What do you think of that?'

'...and Craig?'

'Yes. If you want to be a good mum to Craig you'd learn to do it well. But your way doesn't have to be exactly like someone else's. You learn the bits of parenting that matter but there's lots to do your way. Food, rules and that. You get to be an individual too. Does that sound good?'

'Maybe,' she said so I left it at that.

I had given her a lot to think about.

It was early days yet and we spent the next half hour or so weaving our way through the tricky one way system to find the refuge.

CHAPTER NINE

Eventually we reached our destination. It was a big Victorian house in an affluent part of the city. Built of yellow ochre bricks it had big windows on the ground floor, the same but smaller on the first floor.

The entrance was beautifully decorated in coloured tiles on the ground leading to a wide wooden front door that looked thick and sturdy. I noticed it was different to some of the doors of neighbouring properties because it had no stained glass. That obviously wouldn't be appropriate in a refuge I thought, it would be too easy to punch through. The door was solid and sturdy, made with thick Victorian wood and craftsmanship, much more durable.

From the outside it looked like just a very nice, rather affluent, family home. But that was the whole point.

'Am I going to live here?' Kirsty pointed to the house and turned towards me looking incredulous.

'Yes. Lovely isn't it.' I replied. 'Is that alright?'

'Yeah. It's dead posh. I never thought I'd sleep in a house like that.'

'And why not?' I counteracted. 'You're just as good as anyone else.' This was a good example of Kirsty's low self-esteem. Having spent all her life in cramped social housing I guess it should have been no surprise that being somewhere bigger and altogether more grand would feel different to her. I hoped the beauty of the place might help nourish her spirit.

Kirsty agreed. 'S'pose.'

We went up to the front door loaded with Kirsty's bags and announced our arrival via the intercom. Within seconds the door was opened.

'Caz, lovely to see you.' Kurian ushered us in. 'And you must be Kirsty? Let me help you with those bags. Come and have some tea.' Kurian took a bag and ushered us into a sitting room.

Two children, aged about eight or nine, appeared from a corridor, saw the newcomers and asked Kirsty. 'Hey you, got any kids?' Probably realising this could be a difficult issue for Kirsty, Kurian called back. 'They've only just got here!' She looked at them with a mock frown. 'Let people settle in first, there's good lads. I'm sure you'll find out all about her in time. Now, go and play.' The duo shrugged their shoulders and went away.

We took seats on the sofa.

'I'll show you to your room in a little while,' Kurian said. 'I thought you might appreciate some tea first and to meet Daksha, she's staff here too. She cooks for us sometimes. She should have retired a few years ago but we won't let her leave, she makes wonderful biscuits so she has to stay!' Kurian said with a light heart.

'Hello,' A tiny woman with a welcoming smile approached them. She didn't walk easily, it looked like she'd had an accident of some sort, her right leg was particularly slim and her knee seemed fixed at the wrong angle. A special supportive shoe with a particularly deep sole on her right leg allowed her some mobility but walking looked difficult for her. She carried with her a plate of biscuits but at each movement of her right leg the biscuits slid right to the edge. Kurian didn't seem to notice, she was chatting to Kirsty.

I jumped up from my chair, ready to catch the tasty treats, but Daksha righted the plate at the very last minute.

When she took another step the whole drama started again. The biscuits slid so close to the edge of the plate I sat on the edge of my chair ready to leap.

But once again, Daksha righted the plate at the very last minute. I realised I was in the company of a skilled lady. She was obviously aware of her limitations, but had learned to manage them perfectly. Impressive, I thought.

'Daksha you're getting Carey worried about those biscuits,' Kurian laughed. 'It's time you retired. You look like you're struggling.

'I can't retire,' Daksha laughed. 'What would I do all day? Anyway, someone has to keep you lot in order! I've made some biscuits.' As she got closer to me the smell got stronger and more tempting. 'They are Atta biscuits but I've put some spices in them just like my old dad did in the Punjab. Help yourself.' She put the plate on a coffee table within reach of me and Kirsty.

'Thank you.' I bit into one. It was lovely.

'What's in them?' asked Kirsty.

'Atta. It's a different type of flour and cardamom, a spice,' Daksha explained.

'Oh,' Kirsty eyed it warily before biting into it.

'Is it ok?' Daksha asked, waiting for the response before going to get the drinks.

'Yes,' Kirsty replied after a few moments.

Then Daksha relaxed and asked about the drinks. 'Tea or coffee?' Preferences taken, she went back to the kitchen.

'She's wonderful our Daksha,' Kurian explained as her colleague left the room. 'She's been an inspiration to so many women. Anyway, I'll explain how things work here and you can ask any questions. Most women when they find their way here feel a mixture of feelings, from relief to disappointment and sometimes shame. It's never easy to back out of a relationship you had once had such high hopes for. But you'll find a lot of care in this place. We all look after each other, it's very special. We have a few rules that I hope you won't mind sticking with.'

She counted them out on her fingers. 'First, confidentiality, what people say here stays here. We don't want people's private lives spread outside.'

Kirsty nodded agreement.

Kurian counted to two on her fingers. 'Then we have the lights low and TV quiet after eight because many of our mum's share their rooms with their children and we want the kids to go to sleep. Three, we don't give out the telephone number to others, but you can use it in an emergency if you ask staff. Same with the address, so no friends to visit please, but there's plenty of people here to make friends with. Four, curfew at 11pm.'

A nervous smile came across Kirsty's lips, followed by tears.

'Hey, don't worry.' Kurian passed her a box of tissues. 'Everyone starts off here like that, but soon they relax. When they make new friends and see that everyone's in the same boat. There's always someone around to talk to if you want. And anyway, I haven't told you about our best rule yet,' Kurian said with a smile on her face. 'Every Saturday a few of us cook a meal from our own countries, so we all get a taste of food from all over the world. Sometimes its like mine, food from Iran or a curry, and sometimes its just bog standard English food like fish and chips, depending who is doing the cooking. You don't have to join us, but most people do. And that's about it for rules really. Oh, and there's a rota for the washing machine!' she added in a jovial tone and with a smile.

'Sounds great,' Kirsty said, her mood lighter now.

Daksha joined us with the tea.

I sat back and let the women get to know each other. In many circumstances it would have been appropriate to hug a tearful newcomer, your heart goes out to them and you really do care. But like many of us, Kurian and I agreed that the last thing women who have just escaped violence need is physical contact. The compassion of our words and actions would speak volumes for us.

We sat and chatted for a while then Kurian offered to take us to Kirsty's room. She led the way along a corridor and up some stairs to a light, bright, room on the first floor. It looked out over the front of the house and had a washbasin, bed and a place to store clothes.

The whole impression was that it was clean and homely and Kirsty looked quite happy with that. She sat down on the bed and Kurian went to do some work.

'When does Craig get to come here?' Kirsty asked me.

I braced myself. I didn't want Craig to come straight away, I wanted Kirsty to rest first and be sure that she wasn't going back to Trevor. Besides, when a child is on a care order it's not that easy. Big decisions like that are made after consulting with managers and the wider care team. That's a great help for a social worker, it helps stop mistakes being made.

'You've been through a lot lately,' I soothed. 'Looking after a baby is a huge commitment and you need all your strength to do it well. You need to be well rested and clear about how to look after yourself first and once you've shown you can do that, then it'll be time to look at the future. We'll discuss it with managers and everyone else.'

'Oh,' she grumbled and the smile on her lips dropped. 'But I want him to come back now.'

'It's not just my decision, it's something the whole Child Protection Team talks about and agrees at a meeting which you will be invited too. At the moment this is one of those times where you have to get the basics of your life right first,' I explained gently. 'We need to know things like can you cook for yourself? Can you do your share of housework? Can you make good food choices? And another thing, I know this won't necessarily apply to you, but some women for all sorts of reasons go back to the men they've just left. I know that sounds crazy, but it's really hard to leave someone you invested so much time in, and lots of women get lured back to their ex's by promises of change and they go back for another try.'

Kirsty looked up at me incredulous. 'I'm going nowhere near Trev, that pile of shit!'

'Also, not long ago it looked like you were going to throw Craig over the banister at the police station.' I ventured.

'I would never have done that!' She turned to me and shouted, 'that's just your opinion!'

'Yes, it is just an opinion and I totally accept that I might be wrong. I hope I am wrong. But you can see how it looked to those of us who were there on the day. Lots of people who work with you know about that and will ask for you to have time, to show you're really through that bad patch in your life.'

'But I'm not dangerous. I'm not that sort of person!' Kirsty insisted, tears flowing now. 'You don't want me to have Craig back, do you?'

'Yes I do. When the time is right,' I said. 'But when its late at night and you're on your own and a bit lonely, then it can feel like a good idea to give an old romance a second try. And some abusers can be very persuasive.'

'But I'm not even gonna see Trev! Not ever again!'

'I expect that the child protection team will ask for a psychological report on you so they can really get to the bottom of how you react to stress before Craig comes back.'

'What does that mean?' She lifted her gaze to me, eager for the information. 'Do I have to talk to someone?'

'Yes. Maybe more than once. Maybe quite a few times. And if it's agreed at the meeting that we do need a specialist report, I will find a woman, a psychologist. I think it would be wrong under the circumstances to ask you to talk to a bloke. Would that be ok? It is good that we do everything possible to keep Craig safe, and we'll also do our best to help you be a good parent, by setting up a place for you both, so you always have someone to advise you for your first few months. Do you see what I mean?'

'S'pose.' Kirsty curled up on the bed. Her things were still in their carrier bags. She was tired, I could see that, and giving her a baby to look after, a baby who was possibly still traumatised from the experiences of his early days and could be traumatised again if he'd had to leave his current home, sounded like a recipe for failure.

'So there are a few things we need to get sorted first, but we'll get there. Anyway, I'm going back to the office now, and you need a sleep,' I announced. 'I've lots to do. I'll see you later in the week.'

Kirsty responded with a blink of a bleary eyelid, muttered ok and I left, shutting the door gently behind me. Rest was what she needed, I thought.

I'm often asked if I think the child protection rules are too strict, do they stop me from being the way I want as a social worker? The answer is no. It's a great help to be able to talk these things through with other people in detail working with the client at a child protection meeting, for example. Some clients tell one person something and others something else and I felt I couldn't make a safe plan without information from all the people working with a client, not just me. I welcomed the chance to talk as a team.

I always felt that the social worker has a larger say in planning for the child's future and as a representative of the organisation trusted with the authority to get care orders, that was as it should be.

One thing I would have to answer though, was how long should Kirsty wait till having Craig back again?

It was a question I couldn't answer at that time.

I was in the area a few days later so I went to see Kirsty unannounced. I think it's good to do unannounced visits and we have to do some when children are in care. It always helps to see people when they're not expecting you and haven't had time to tidy up or think about what they're going to say. I often think you see more of the real person.

When I arrived Kirsty was in the kitchen having her hair done by another resident who used to be a hairdresser. I won't say she looked deliriously happy, there was still a lot of sadness in her expression. But she looked calmer than I had ever seen her. I suppose you'd expect that since she was a different place now. She didn't ask about Craig though. Odd that, I thought.

But it was what happened a few days later that worried me. I had a call when I was in the office on the Monday morning following her arrival at the refuge, that I wasn't expecting.

'I'm ringing about Kirsty,' Kurian explained. 'We had her ex, Trevor, visit last night about 1am. He was drunk, shouting and bawling, demanding to see Kirsty. We had to get the police.' I could hear the concern in her voice.

'Why? What happened?' My tummy tensed with anxiety. I was just starting to believe maybe Kirsty could be a parent. Was I about to learn how wrong I was?

'Kirsty was in bed at the time,' Kurian continued. 'Her room overlooks the entrance as you know, and the noise and commotion in the street woke people up. We had one of the relief staff on that night and she wasn't sure whether Kirsty had invited him or not, so she was very wary of her. Kirsty woke up and came running downstairs in floods of tears, shaking like a leaf. She was trying to open the front door and was apparently very rude when stopped. The relief worker got really anxious, she's fairly new and to my mind didn't handle it well. She was anxious and panicky herself and that made the situation worse.'

'It would do. So was Kirsty trying to get to Trevor?' I asked, hoping to hear the answer I wanted yet trying to keep an open mind.

'Well, maybe. It could be that way. But...' Kurian spoke thoughtfully.

'How did he know where she was?' I asked.

'We've never been able to keep our address totally secret, there have always been some people who do tell others where we are. But the relief thinks Kirsty might have told him. I don't think she has any reason for that though, it's just guesswork. We did ask Kirsty but she insists she didn't. The relief worker just says she would say that wouldn't she, and maintains Kirsty is being less than truthful.'

'Oh what a pain. I'll come over and see her,' I agreed.

I rang the police to hear their side of the story and found out that Trevor had been arrested and charged with harassment and as he has several bail conditions already, he wasn't allowed bail. Having gleaned all the facts I spoke to Graham and Trish who agreed I needed to ask Kirsty what had happened.

Fortunately my diary was pretty empty that morning so I was at the refuge in half an hour. Kirsty was lying on the bed curled up like a baby, eyes puffy with tears and looking very tense. How did Trevor know where she was? Had she told him? Did she even ask him to come? All these questions swirled around in my brain.

I sat in a chair next to her. 'Poor you! You've had a rotten time,' I sympathised. 'Tell me exactly what happened.'

Kirsty spoke with difficulty, gulping and sobbing between words, 'I...I... was up here asleep. I went to bed early because I was tired. I was really sound asleep and when I heard this shoutin'. I took no notice at first. Then I recognised the voice. Trev. He was outside shoutin' 'Kirst..Kirst, open this fuckin' door now!'...then he started bashing it. I expect he was kicking it cos he always kicks things. He was gonna wake everyone up and there's little kids here and some of my mates here have to get up for school the next day and I know Jo had a job interview so she needed a good nights sleep. I couldn't let him wake them up. So I went downstairs to sort him out. I was gonna open the door and tell him to piss off, then this relief woman called Gill came in, saw what I was doin' and had a right go at me.'

'Eh?' I furrowed my brow.

'She said I had no rights to open the door. She said staff always deal with visitors at this time of night and I was to get away from it and go back to my room. Well, I didn't know only staff do that did I? And it was middle of the night. I didn't even know if staff were awake or not.'

'I see what you mean. What happened next?'

'I went upstairs cos she shouted at me, I told her she was a bitch cos she didn't listen to me. I was well pissed off. And a few of the others came up to see me cos I said I was gonna get out right now. I said it's not on the way she shouted at me and I wasn't putting up with it...'

'Others? Which others?' I queried. Could she mean other blokes? I so hoped not.

'Sammy and Jo and a few more. They're here with their kids too.'

'Ah, I see. You mean other residents here,' I said with relief.

'Yeah. I said I wanted to go now, even if it was the middle of the night and I started packing my bags.' She swept her newly trimmed hair away from her eyes. 'I told my mates I was going and they went to tell Gill, but Gill didn't believe them. She said I had come down to see him and she said cos I wanted to leave that proved it. But it didn't. And anyway he had been taken away by police.'

'How did you feel when they turned up to take him away?' I asked.

'Shit!' Kirsty looked at me shocked. 'Cos now all my mates knew he was here and I had Gill goin' on at me cos she thought I wanted to talk to him in a nice way. I didn't, I was gonna give him a mouthful!'
I could see how Gill might think Kirsty had gone to open the door for Trevor. I nodded in sympathy. 'What a horrible thing to go through. But how did he know where to find you?'

'I don't know. Kurian keeps asking that.'

'Have you had any contact with Trev?' I had to ask. Could I trust her reply? We were planning a child's future here. If I believed her and we let her take Craig home and she took Craig to see violent Trevor... well, I didn't dare think what could happen. But she seemed to be honest and her story did make sense. Even if she had done the wrong thing she hadn't been here very long and could easily have not known how things work.

'I wouldn't speak to him if you paid me! But I was gonna' tell him to piss off, I'd have liked that.' She sat up on the bed and looked straight at me. 'I bet you won't let me have Craig back now, will you?'

'I didn't say that. I believe you. But it's not just my decision as you know...'

'... it's the whole child protection meeting blah, blah, blah. Don't tell me, I know.'

'You got it,' I replied, ignoring her flippant tone.

'And they'll say no, I know, I know.' Her gaze questioned me.

'Not necessarily. They will take other things into account, like how you are between now and the next meeting and probably what the psychologist says, if they decide to use one. They might really insist, and give you no choice on you going to a mother and baby placement with a foster carer first, so you can learn to look after Craig properly.'

'What's that again?'

"Its where you stay with a foster carer with Craig, to learn about him. What do you think of that?'

'S'pose.' I could see the tension in her muscles relax a bit. I thought that was a good sign. 'So can I see Craig then?' There was a hint of excitement in her gaze.

'Yes, as long as my boss says it's ok, at the family centre again.'

'I knew it. There's always some reason why I don't get my way.' She turned towards her pillow and groaned. 'I don't know why I even believed in you.'

'Look.' I crouched down to her side to explain. 'It isn't that I don't believe you, I do. But the child protection machine is very cautious. I would even say over cautious. And it's not always right, I know that. But it is about as safe a system as you can ever get. I know it must be frustrating for you, and I'm sure it hurts like hell. But just stick with it. You're doing fine, honest.'

Kirsty was looking up at me, eyes wide open, welling up with tears.

I couldn't promise her she'd have Craig back. What if she had encouraged Trev? But I had to give her enough hope to carry on.

'Look, I have to go now to see someone else. I'll come and see you later in the week,' I said, and left the room.

Kirsty nodded a weak goodbye.

So was I right or was I wrong to believe her?

Only time would tell, and I was pleased the ultimate decision about letting Craig live with her or not would be made by all of us who work with her, not just me.

CHAPTER TEN

The next time we had contact, which I supervised, things didn't go according to plan. I had collected Craig and taken him to the family centre in my car and Kirsty had caught the bus and we met at the family centre and we met there. He was in his special car seat asleep most of the time and for the short time he was awake he didn't seem interested in anything that was going on around him. But he's young, over five months now and it had been over three weeks since Kirsty had seen him, which I guess was quite a long time in a baby's life.

I felt sorry for Kirsty. She did her best and chatted away to him but he just didn't want to know and went to sleep.

I would have to write that in my notes, but babies can be difficult, they sleep when you want them awake and vice versa. The fact that Craig was sleeping now wasn't Kirsty's fault. But a contact supervisor is expected to gain some understanding of the interaction between mother and child to write down in a fairly detailed format which can then be submitted to the court and other relevant parties.

It's really important to be non-biased in a report, but in practice it's quite hard to do. Courts always employ a Guardian ad Litem, a guardian in law, who will read every document, speak to all involved, and produce their own independent report for the court to get over that problem.

So we sat and chatted for the last half hour of the contact, with Kirsty next to Craig asleep in his car seat, looking angelic as his features were filling out even more now his meals were more regular and he was losing the dull, grey tinge to his skin he'd when he was very stressed.

The second supervised contact was shortly before the child protection meeting. Craig was awake and quite cheerful. He smiled when his mother picked him up. This really seemed to strike a chord with Kirsty, she snuggled him close to her and chatted away to him about what they were going to do in the future and how she'd teach him to ride a bike and cook him nice dinners. He laughed and she laughed back. It was a delightful scene, I just kept out of the way and took notes.

The following day it was the Child Protection Meeting. I'd gone through my report with Kirsty the day before. She arrived ten minutes early having got the bus to my office. Val rang me on my desk phone and told me she'd arrived. She had told me she hadn't wanted to go to these meetings so I was quite surprised to see her here. They do feel intimidating, frightening places for those who aren't used to them.

People say they feel judged and overwhelmed and I suspected that was the case with Kirsty, although I had done my best to reassure her she'd nothing to fear.

I went to the office door to let her in. Val looked over to me with a broad smile, I know that was to say how much better Kirsty was now than on her previous visits.

Kirsty looked nervous, tiny, slim, pale. I stood holding the door open behind me to welcome her in. I could see fear in her eyes, which was only natural since we were making important decisions about her son. 'It's nice to see you. I thought you weren't going to be able to make it.'

'Well, I got somethin' to say,' she muttered, but there was a sense of purpose in her voice that I hadn't heard before. 'I thought if I don't say it myself it won't come over right.'

I was going to ask her what it was, but Nitin, chair of the meeting, interrupted us.

'Excuse me, are you Craig's mother?' he asked with a welcoming smile.

She looked round at me as if asking if it was ok to speak to him.

'Yes,' I quickly responded. 'This is Nitin, who is going to Chair the meeting. He likes to introduce himself to the family before the meeting because it helps them to be less nervous,' I explained.

'That's right I do, and I'm really pleased you were able to make it.'

He welcomed Kirsty, with a friendly smile and held out his hand to shake which she did gingerly. 'These meetings always go better when the family are here. Would you like to come with me and I'll explain how it all works?' He gestured the direction and went off with Kirsty whilst I returned to my desk to gather my notes.

It wasn't much longer till everyone had arrived and taken their seat in the conference room. Graham was the only manager with me as Trish was away. The police hadn't joined us but they had sent a message to say that Trevor has been charged with harassment for the car park incident. Kirsty was going to get a caution, because while she didn't take much active part, she was there confirming my identity to Trevor. But since Craig was safe now, police were waiting to hear what Dr Gladstone said about any further charges in respect of Craig. But she hadn't completed her report yet because she wanted to see how Craig developed before deciding whether they wanted to press charges for neglect or similar on Kirsty. I wouldn't be in favour of that. If it was ever floated as an idea I'd be arguing against it. Kirsty was very low at that time and not her usual self, I was sure.

We also had an extra two attendees, Kurian as representative of the refuge and Hazel who worked at the Family Centre and had been allocated to work with Kirsty.

We took our seats, me next to Kirsty. Nitin moved on to the formal part of the meeting. He began with the rules, standard practice but useful for Kirsty since it was her first attendance at any sort of meeting like this. It was followed with a round of introductions. 'One rule I'd like to remind everyone of is the need to speak when invited by myself only. It may be that you will hear something you'd like to challenge, but please wait to be asked and I will invite you to speak in turn. First we'll hear from Carey. I believe there have been considerable changes since we last met.'

I went through my report, summarising what had happened until now. 'Kirsty has been at the refuge five weeks and there has been one incident in which Trevor tried to see her. The police were called and Trevor was arrested. He has been charged with harassment with bail conditions not to approach Kirsty, which so far, we believe he has complied with since that Sunday night recently. We don't know how he got the address of the refuge but police are looking into it. We have had two contact visits between mother and son, one which didn't go so well because Craig slept through it and a second that went very well. On that occasion mother and son were enjoying each other's company so my conclusion is that we should explore Kirsty's ability to parent Craig, but cautiously, probably with a mother and baby placement at a foster carers as the next step. I'd also like to ask for a psychologists report to look at the issues of safety for Craig following the balcony incident and relationship issues. Kirsty has had a poor experience of parenting herself and it would be useful to have a look at that too with a specialist psychologist being asked to prepare a report on that. I have discussed this with Kirsty and she is in agreement. The waiting time for a hearing at the court is so long we can fit it in without delaying the procedures, if we still need them.'

'Thank you, Carey. Now, as we usually do we'll ask everyone else how the past few months have been.' Nitin invited Sally the Health visitor to speak first.

'I visited Craig at his foster carers. There's no doubt he has suffered and his development appears to be delayed but he is improving at the moment. To be quite honest I'm not sure about his mother, and how much she should be involved in his future care. Craig needs someone reliable and consistent, and I'm not sure Kirsty is that person.'

Kirsty glared over at the woman and I felt her take a deep breath and lunge forward, probably to shout out. I put my hand on her forearm to stop her.

Nitin noticed and turned to Kirsty. 'There will be some comments that I know will be difficult for you to hear. But as I explained, only by getting to know these issues will we be able to deal with them. Have patience and you will have your turn to speak.'

Kirsty sat back in her chair.

'Thank you, Sally. We'll hear from Hazel, Kirsty's worker at the Family Centre next,' Nitin stated, looking in Hazel's direction.

'Thanks,' Hazel began. 'I can second what Caz said. Kirsty always seems to be interested in what we do and why. I had a very interesting conversation with her after Caz had left last week. I showed her all the groups we do for parents, Coping with Tantrums, My Child Won't Eat, Friday Fun for Under Fives, and she was very keen to attend, which I thought was very positive. I'd like to see Kirsty and Craig in a mother and baby placement, I think Kirsty could learn and has more to give.'

Then it was the turn of the Refuge Manager, Kurian. 'We have seen a change in Kirsty in the few weeks she's been with us. There have been no more incidents like the one we had with Trevor, thank goodness. When she first arrived she didn't do much cooking and stayed in her room a lot. I thought that was depression and we got her registered with a GP, which Carey suggested, and I took her to see the doctor. She said she's not surprised she's depressed when she heard Kirsty's history and gave her some tablets and they do seem to have helped. Now Kirsty has made friends with a couple of other women we have living with us who also have children and she spends a lot of time with them. She seems much happier. I think she's ready for a mother and baby placement now. Other than being safe, we aren't the sort of place where Kirsty can learn much about parenting except what she sees in other residents.'

'Thank you, Kurian.

'Maya, you speak for the adoption and fostering team, would you like to speak next?'

'Thank you, Nitin. I have had a long discussion with Janet, she is happy to provide a mother and baby placement for Kirsty and Craig which would save him going anywhere else obviously. But in terms of an extra report from a psychologist, I'm in favour of that. It's a big decision so we need to have every bit of information possible.'

'Thank you, Maya. Now Kirsty, would you like to say your part?' Nitin invited her.

Kirsty stood up, which wasn't really expected but nobody minded. She looked nervous, threading the papers she'd been given through her hands. She took a deep breath and cleared her throat.

'I know I got off to a bad start with Craig, I can't deny that. But I know what I done was wrong and I wanna change. I thought Trev would be a good dad cos at first he was really good with kids. He seemed nice and kind. I can see now that was an act, I just couldn't see it at the time. I don't think I wanted to see it at first, to be honest. I thought I'd met someone really special and I just had to put up with his moods. But when things got worse and Carey said basically it was either Trev or Craig I couldn't stay with him no more. And when I got to the refuge and I met others who had been through the same thing, I realised I'd been taken for a ride. That won't happen again. I'm really pleased Carey let me see Craig. But I told myself not to love him too much in case I wasn't allowed to have him. But I couldn't help it. He was so sweet. I buried my nose in his tummy and breathed in his lovely baby smell. Now I wanna do whatever I need to to be a good mum. I know if I want to have Craig back I'll have to change and I'll do that. Anything. Just give me a chance. Please.'

Kirsty looked around and seemed to see for the first time how many people were in the room, each of them listening to her, their concentration total. I expected her to stop at this point, now that she'd seen her audience. But rather than spook her it seemed to give her renewed energy.

She cleared her throat and carried on. 'I didn't tell Kurian but I never took those depression tablets. I don't wanna get so used to them that I can't get off of them. I wanna be a good mum, without tablets. I saw some mums down the park, their children were running round playing chase. They watched the kids but at the same time they was chatting and havin' a good time. I wanna be like that. I want to make friends and go round each other's houses. I wanna change nappies and make up milk bottles like I know what I was doing. Carey said I might be able to stay with Craig in the foster carer's house and learn to look after him properly. And that's what I want to do.' She looked around nervously and said 'well, that's it really,' and sat down.

Everyone looked moved even though they tried to maintain a position of professional neutrality. Several people thanked her for her honesty, and others just smiled in her direction.

'That was very well put,' Nitin said and turned to Kirsty. 'Obviously we do have things we need to talk about and plans we need to make in respect of Craig and yourself now.'

'You're gonna decide whether I can have him or not, aren't you?' Kirsty replied, looking at Nitin with concern. I could almost hear her heart throbbing away frantically at the possibility that the next few minutes might go against her.

'It's a big decision for the meeting,' Nitin replied, his expression giving away nothing.

'Please give me a chance,' Kirsty pleaded and turned towards the group looking at each member in turn. 'If I'm crap I'll let you get him adopted cos he needs a family, I know that. But I'll show you how good I can be. Please.'

The meeting attendees nodded in a non-committed way.

'That was a very eloquent speech Kirsty, thank you for that. If you follow you'll know the reason for our decision, if you wouldn't mind listening at first, we'll give you time to speak later.' Nitin turned to the other meeting attendees. 'What are your thoughts? I must admit I hadn't come here with the intention of changing our plans for a Care Order followed by adoption. But I am quite willing to continue with that if it's seen as in Craig's best interests.'

'Can I start?' Sally the Health Visitor began. 'Because I know that was an excellent and very moving little speech. But you can't make a decision on words alone. I am worried about Kirsty with Craig and I don't mind saying it. It's not long ago that she seemed willing to throw the poor little mite over a balcony and maybe even herself too. That could have killed him or at least done him some permanent damage. It's is a very serious thing to do and it makes me question whether she should be allowed to have Craig, or any child even, in an unsupervised setting. And the condition Craig was in when I saw him at Janet's was appalling. He had nappy rash, he'd obviously missed meals, there were bruises on him. Somebody had neglected him and possibly worse and it was Kirsty's job to care for him at that time. What if she feels depressed again? Babies are not easy to look after, they are exhausting, time consuming and sometimes downright difficult. Janet has worked wonders with him, with her patience and skill. Craig is older now and has a sense of place. Research says that when babies are adopted, and I know if Kirsty isn't going to have him he would be adopted, he'll adjust quicker the younger he is when he's placed. I don't want him to wait any longer. It wouldn't be fair on him to wait, whilst we decide whether Kirsty is up to the job or not?'

'But that's not…' Kirsty pulled an angry face and squirmed in her chair.

Nitin held up his hand to her to stop her speaking. 'In a minute.'

'I know what you mean,' Kurian added. 'It's Craig we need to consider as a priority here. I worry if Kirsty can sustain her resolve? Would she feel the same after hours, days even, of a baby crying that she didn't know how to deal with? It is lovely having a child, but when it's not well, or you've got bills coming at you thick and fast and piles of washing that seems never ending, it could be a different thing.'

I shuddered. I could see that, I really could. But how fair is it to judge someone when they're at their lowest? Was it really her lowest or was she often like that? This meeting was going badly. I needed to put the opposite point of view.

Could I turn this meeting around singlehandedly? Should I even try? May be they were right, keeping Craig away from Kirsty and putting him with adoptive parents was the safest option. Most adoptive families are well resourced, kind and considerate people. There was no doubt that that was the safest way forward.

But what was right for Craig?

CHAPTER ELEVEN

'I take those points, I really do,' I argued. 'But if you had seen mother and son together at contact the second time you would see how totally happy they were, how completely wrapped up they were in each other and enjoying every second of their time together. I realise that thinking about being a parent and actually being a parent is very different in the harsh light of day. But which of us hasn't got themselves tied up in a relationship they later regret? Especially when young.' I looked from one attendee to another. We'd had enough chats in the staff room for me to know the truth of my words.

I continued. 'I suspect the underlying pathology is an attachment disorder, that Kirsty's own parenting was so poor she was looking for a relationship to supplement her early experiences. Now I'm not one to take risks, especially with the wellbeing of a child, but I do think there is a way we can try this without exposing Craig to harm. If we use Janet as a mother and baby placement there is minimal risk to Craig, minimal disruption and support for Kirsty. That would provide her with a family, albeit short term, in a healthy way.'

There was a pause for a moment.

'Janet would be quite happy with that,' Maya added. 'She's often said she'd like another mother and baby placement. She hasn't had one for a while. I also think a separate, independent report from a psychologist is a good idea, so we have an extra specialist point of view.'

'We can arrange for Kirsty to stay longer at the refuge whilst it's done,' Kurian added.

'That's good to know,' I acknowledged. I held my breath. I knew there was an element of risk, but I just felt it was the right thing to do for Craig. I could feel the tension in my muscles as we waited for the next person to speak.

Kirsty sat on the edge of her seat, gripping the documents in her hand so hard it turned her knuckles white. 'Please. Please!' she implored in a whisper.

Nitin ignored her. 'Are we all agreed that a psychologist's report on Kirsty is a good idea?' he asked. 'Several teams I know have used one particular person and she has been very good. I believe she has some space to work quickly too because she's just completed a large piece of work.'

'I agree with the mother and baby placement plan too. The specialist report is also an excellent suggestion, Nitin,' Graham replied.

'I will have to ask for some money from senior managers for the extra cost of the placement, but if this meeting recommends it, there shouldn't be a problem. The way these things work is extras like this aren't provided until you ask. But when a child is on an interim care order money will have to be found, because unless we try these ideas the court might not be willing to make an order anyway. We might have to let Kirsty have a chance. It's possible she may not meet the criteria for a care order at the moment whilst these chances are possible anyway.'

'How would you feel about that, Kirsty?' Nitin asked. 'A psychologist would visit you then write a report on you and if the conclusion of that was positive you could go to a mother and baby placement, say, for about three months? It will involve you not taking him out alone at first.'

'Well, I want him now, why can't I have him now? He is my son!' Kirsty pleaded, tears brimming over. 'Everyone knows I don't see Trev no more and I have changed a lot. I don't wanna see this other person I just want Craig.'

'I totally see what you mean Kirsty,' I pointed out kindly. 'But we're making major decisions here about a child's future. What we do now will affect him for the rest of his life. If we make a mistake it could damage him forever.'

'I think that's an excellent idea,' Sally the health visitor chimed in. Others agreed too.

Kirsty frowned. 'So what you're saying is I've got to see this psycho…person then?'

'Psychologist. Yes. That's right.' I replied, trying to avoid a debate with Kirsty but just explain. 'Think of it this way, it's not a complete no.'

Kirsty sighed in despair. 'Oh, ok. Let's get on with it then. I'll do it.'

'I don't think we should go ahead with the placement until we have the psychologist's report.' The Health Visitor frowned. 'We could be creating a stronger bond between the two and need to part them at a later date.'

'That's a good point. We need to delay Kirsty moving to the mother and baby placement straight away, until we've had the psychologists report, because if the report finds something worrying the whole plan might have to be changed,' Graham proposed.

Kirsty shouted and glaring straight ahead thrust her body back in her chair in irritation. 'Well what could she find wrong? Answer me that?' It's just another thing to stop me having Craig isn't it? I thought you was on my side!'

I replied calmly, no stranger to having my plans challenged by clients. 'I'm on Craig's side, if you want to put it like that. It's because not that long ago that you appeared to be wanting to throw him over a balcony and you weren't looking after him very well. That's why. We don't know your real inner motives, so we are bound to be cautious.'

'I would never do anything to hurt Craig! I told you. I was not going to do that!' Kirsty replied in anger. 'And he is my baby! I'm missing all his baby stages!'

'The fact that he's your baby doesn't prove that you are able to care for him properly. We see plenty of parents who aren't able to look after their children. I'm not saying I don't believe in you, Kirsty. I do. Looking at you now I can see that you're totally committed, you really, really want to look after Craig. But parenting involves a lot of hard work, it's about waking in the night when you're desperately tired, about spending your last penny on nourishing food for him, and dealing with a stressful child when you've plenty of stress of your own. I get your concern, I really do. I can see that what we want is a big ask. But when we're dealing with children everything needs to be as safe as possible. I'm just asking you to prove your side of the bargain.'

Kirsty groaned in resignation. 'How many more things are you going to find to stop me! Oh, I s'pose. If I have to then.'

'Thank you,' I spoke with relief. 'The psychologist should be able to do the work quickly, if not we'll find another, so it should be done within a month and we can make a decision then,' Nitin explained.

'Well, can I see him more often?'

'No. We'll stick with twice a week as it is.'

'But that's not enough!' Kirsty frowned.

'If we do have to look elsewhere for someone else to bring him up, we don't want him to be too fond of you. We can't help the fact that he'll be fond of his foster carers, but we need to keep you at arms length for the time being. Is that alright?'

'It'll have to be won't it?' Kirsty spoke with resignation. 'I haven't got a choice have I?'

'Well done,' I enthused.

'Sally the Health Visitor spoke next. 'I can see the wisdom in that plan.' Her words were quickly followed by agreements from the rest of the group.

'So does everyone agree with the proposal for Kirsty to have a psychologist's intervention to assess her risk to her son and for Craig, and Kirsty to go to Janet's as a mother and baby placement if the conclusion of the report is favourable?' Nitin looked around at the attendee's, quizzing their expressions for a response. 'Kirsty must understand that it is not necessarily a plan for her to have Craig.'

Kirsty nodded reluctantly.

'I think we can get the report done within the next month,' Graham said. 'We'll be commissioning the psychologist privately so there won't be a waiting list. And if a small core group of us could convene at the end of the month, we should have the document and can complete the next stage of our planning then as a small group.' Graham looked around at everyone at the meeting.

'I quite agree with that. I'll remind Kirsty she has one chance and one chance only,' I agreed.

'One thing, I'd like it added to the minutes and for Kirsty to acknowledge, we won't tolerate any breaches of conditions,' Graham said. 'It doesn't matter what the excuse is, if Kirsty slips up once and comes back drunk or invites loads of people around to drink or do drugs or whatever, that will be the end of it and we'll search for a family to adopt him. She needs to know that.'

I could see the tension in Kirsty's expression. 'Yes I understand. I can do that.'

People nodded agreement, their serious expressions underlining the gravity of the situation.

'So if we have Sally, Carey, Kurian, Graham, Maya and Trish to meet at the end of the month is that ok?' The plan was agreed then. 'Of course we'll be loosing Kurian after that because Kirsty will be leaving the refuge. Do I assume you'd all prefer Craig's name to remain on the Child Protection Register, since his future is uncertain?'

People lifted their hands in agreement.

'That is unanimous then. I think we can draw this meeting to a close,' Nitin gathered papers into his briefcase.

I turned to speak to Kirsty but quick as a flash she was off out of the door and gone. That was strange I thought. I get that she was cross, things hadn't gone exactly her way, but I would have thought she'd want to talk things over afterwards.

I just hoped my confidence in her wasn't misplaced.

CHAPTER TWELVE

The next three weeks passed slowly. I had asked the family centre to supervise the contact because Trish said it freed me up for more child protection work so I didn't see Kirsty much.

I engaged the psychologist and asked her to particularly look at whether Kirsty meant to throw her son over the balcony or not on that day. We just had to wait for the results.

I had reports from the family centre saying that Kirsty was always on time for contact, that Craig seemed to enjoy seeing her and she played with him with appropriate toys. They had given her some guidance as to what things he'd like according to his age, which was fine. They'd also said that Kirsty eagerly read the posters on the wall about diet, sleep and other advice.

It was a good start, but on its own not enough.

Sooner than I expected we had the report and I arranged a meeting with Sally, Maya, Graham, the psychologist, myself and Kirsty.

The psychologist, Anita, began with a verbal summary of her report.

'Kirsty has issues with angry men because she was bought up with an angry father for the early part of her childhood and I believe that is partly why she has chosen her partners badly. Angry men will have felt familiar to her, comfortable almost. She will have lacked the self-esteem to walk away. People who are abused absorb a view of themselves that is completely wrong, they typically see themselves as worthless. They don't feel important. They believe that if anyone has hurt them, that somehow they deserved it. It's very hard for people to unlearn that. So it's not uncommon for people who have had that sort of experience to have a track record of poor relationships.

'I think the fact that Kirsty ran away from her mother and is no longer in contact with her shows a willingness to break away from the lifestyle her mother had created. It's logical that she has nothing to replace it with, no role models to show her a better way of life, no skills in being either an adult or a mother. I think what she needs is, for want of a better phrase, a role model in mothering. Someone to show her how to bring up a baby, how to cook for a child, how to deal with tantrums and the inevitable problems life will throw up. I think a mother and baby placement will provide for this perfectly. If I might also suggest a few counselling sessions from myself to help her thoroughly distance herself from previous relationship styles, then we would see a totally different person in Kirsty for the future.'

I breathed a sigh of relief and looked around at the rest of the group who, guessing by their facial expressions, seemed to be thinking something similar.

'To answer your question, Carey,' the psychologist explained handing out a copy for each of us of the report. 'I don't think Kirsty had planned to throw Craig over the balcony on that day. But she had manoeuvred herself into that dangerous corner to get away from authority. Once that was done it had occurred to her only as a possibility during that altercation. Whether she could have brought herself to do that in reality, I very, very much doubt.'

I looked round at Kirsty. She was crying.

'I thought you'd be happy about that Kirst?' I was puzzled.

'I am happy about that,' she sniffed. 'It's was just such a crap thing to go through. Before I started seeing a social worker I thought it was normal. Now I know it wasn't.'

I touched her forearm briefly in support. I looked at Graham, delighted with the report and eager to give Kirsty and Craig the opportunity to work towards the life together they both deserved. But there was still one problem, funding for the mother and baby placement, it still hadn't been agreed since there was an element of insecurity in the plan. Everything boiled down to money with the local authority, strapped for cash as they always were.

I turned to Graham. 'It sounds like just the opportunity Craig needs, but it will cost a lot. Can we go for it?' I looked up at him open eyed, almost pleading with him to agree.

'Yes. I think the managers will go for that,' Graham acknowledged. 'The cost of a mother and baby placement plus some counselling sessions is considerable. But in the long term it's cheaper than keeping a child in care, even though that would be reasonably short term since adoption is likely. I also think that unless we give Kirsty the chance to parent since she's shown interest, it's very likely the judge in any court wouldn't make a care order anyway unless we'd given it a try. But we must do it quickly, because every day Craig gets older he'll find it harder to adapt to a new family if that's what we need in the end.'

'So you all agree to Kirsty going to Janet's as soon as possible?' I asked.

'Yes, we agree with that,' the attendee's said individually.

'It is good,' I explained slowly, not allowing too many signs of excitement to creep into my voice or manner. 'It says that, in a nutshell, there were things in your childhood that stopped you being able to judge the men in your life properly. Basically, you should just have walked away from some men, Trev amongst them. Easier said than done though, I'm sure.'

'Don't I know it,' her eyes welled up. 'How about Craig? When am I allowed to have him.'

'Once the funding has been sorted and Janet is ready. It is a big step forward though and I am pleased for you. But be careful. If you falter, well, you'll lose Craig. You have one chance and one chance only,' my words might have sounded harsh, but Kirsty needed to be in no doubt of her choices.

I saw Kirsty pale as she digested the enormity of what I was saying. 'So you're saying I can't mess up?'

'That's right.'

'But that's more than you'd ask of any other parent isn't it?' There was a note of accusation in her voice.

I could see what she meant, so I gave her a few real stories. 'I know someone else in this position a few months ago. Left the baby with the foster carer without telling her, went to the pub, came back drunk. Another woman met her dangerous boyfriend thinking she could keep it secret and got found out. Both women lost their babies. Stability and 100% commitment is what every baby and child needs. It's what Craig deserves. That's the flip side of parenting, especially single parenting, it is lovely having a baby and going out to lunch with other mums. But usually behind every happy baby is a totally committed and very often exhausted parent.'

I could see her weighing up the prospect as I spoke. 'I really can't mess up can I?'

'No. I like you, I believe in you, I think you have what it takes to be a great mum. But I want Craig to have a great childhood. I hope that's with you but…' I shrugged my shoulders and let her think.

Kirsty nodded slowly. I could see her computing the reality.

'How often would I see him if he was adopted?' Kirsty asked.

'Not at all. Once he's adopted no more visits. We'd be asking for no contact so Craig can get fully integrated into his new family. You can write him a letters and we keep those in the office and he can ask for them when he's older, but that's it.'

'It's scary.' Her expression reflected the gravity of my words.

'But there are some good points.' I lightened my tone. 'As far as possible to do we're going to teach you what you should have learnt as a child. You'll stay with Janet in your own room, that has its own kitchen and bathroom. She'll cook for you at first but after that you cook for yourself and prepare food for Craig. You'll have a series of six

95

counselling sessions from the psychologist to help you see what you missed in your childhood and how to avoid having unhelpful people in your life.'

'Sounds good.' Kirsty relaxed a little.

'Janet will be there all the time and show you what to do and answer any questions you have, but the primary responsibility for Craig is yours. There are various groups at the family centre that you and he can go to in time. We want you to stay in with Craig and Janet for his first two weeks, and we don't want Trevor to know where you are. Ever. When its time for you both to leave, we'll find you a place to live together.'

'That sounds ok,' Kirsty looked relieved.

'Yes. We're not setting you up to fail, we're setting you up to win and giving you all the skills you'll need to be a mum. But I just need you to know exactly what happens if…well, you know. I'm sure I don't need to go over it again, do I?' I looked over at Kirsty, with seriousness in my gaze.

'I know. I get it. Mess up, no Craig. I'm just so pleased you gave me another chance. I won't mess it up Caz, honestly I won't.'

'Good. I'm pleased to hear it. So is Thursday morning ok for you to move to Janet's? Maya will check she's ok about that but she's already knows it was a probability.'

'Yes!' Kirstie shrieked with happiness and punched the air.

'I'll pick you up Thursday morning then,' I smiled as I left her room.

CHAPTER THIRTEEN

Kirsty looked completely different when I picked her up on Thursday.

'Daksha took me to a charity store that has a whole store of old clothes and let me choose some for me and some for Craig too. Do you like this dress?' She held her arms out to her side and spun round as a fashion model might.

'You look fab!' I said truthfully. Somehow, she looked brighter. Or maybe it was just the prospect of her new life that was making her look so different. We took her few bags to the car ready to go to Janet's.

'And I've got some lovely things for Craig,' Kirsty said as she settled into the passenger seat. She scrabbled about in a bag and laid a few new to her baby clothes on her lap to show me before I started the car. The things she had chosen were really charming, in various colours, some bearing jaunty slogans others with little pictures on. I glanced over before we pulled away.

'They're gorgeous!' I enthused.

'It's just so nice to be able to look after him myself now.' She folded the clothes neatly and put them back in the bag.

'I'm sure it must be.' I crossed my fingers hoping she would still feel the same when woken in the middle of the night or early in the morning and she had to get up when she was already exhausted..

We pulled up outside Janet's house and Kirsty sat silent, mouth wide open.

'What's the matter?' I asked following her gaze. 'Don't you like it?'

'Yeah.' She took a deep breath. 'Am I gonna stay there? It's like the refuge, posh!"

'I suppose it is. I guess it's because they are big houses that can fit a lot of people in, so that's why they're chosen when looking for housing for more than one small family.' I looked at the house myself. I had seen it many times before but I tried to see it how Kirsty saw it. It was quite big and imposing. Built I guess in the 1970's with its own driveway and main entrance plus a side entrance it probably could be quite intimidating if you were only used to small houses. 'You'll be here probably about two or three months I imagine, then we'll see what social housing is available for you.'

That was the last sensible word I got out of Kirsty, for the next half hour or so. Janet opened the door holding Craig and Kirsty was beyond herself with excitement. She ran up to him and Janet passed the baby to his mother who took him a little bit awkwardly, but very enthusiastically.

'Oh how I've missed you!' Kirsty shrieked and held him close. The baby looked around for Janet and when he saw she'd walked away his bottom lip trembled and he looked on the verge of tears. Kirsty noticed and tried to ignore it as she snuggled him close to her and kissed him over and over again but Craig just looked distressed and began to cry, reaching out towards Janet, I felt for Kirsty.

'He's ready for a bottle,' Janet stepped towards him to soothe him. 'I thought you'd like to give it to him, but it meant making him wait a little longer. I'm sorry, it's meant he was hungry and grumpy.'

I looked at Kirsty. I could see the disappointment in her eyes. Craig was holding his arms out to Janet asking her to take him.

'No, sausage,' Janet held his little hand briefly. 'You're with your mother now. Let's go and get your bottle, shall we?'

We went into the kitchen and Janet got the milk for Craig. He sucked it readily.

Kirsty looked upset, and a large tear ran down her cheek, followed by another and another.

'I'm sorry it's not gone as you'd hoped.' Janet noticed and soothed Kirsty, resting her hand on her shoulder briefly. 'It isn't because he doesn't care for you. It's just how things are now. It won't always be like that.'

I added my bit. 'This won't be in the report,' I explained softly. 'It's a transition stage so it doesn't show how things will always be in the future. Some confusion for Craig is bound to happen.'

'It wouldn't have happened if you hadn't taken him off of me in the first place would it?' Kirsty propped the bottle under her chin and whisked her tears away quickly with the back of her hand.

'You weren't in your right mind at the time, it didn't look like you were well enough to look after a baby.' I reminded her in reassuring tones.

'I had looked after him since he was born. I could still have done it!' Kirsty grumbled.

Craig frowned and looked concerned, but he was too busy with his bottle to cry. Kirsty looked at him tenderly.

'Your life was completely different then to how it is now,' I reminded her gently. 'You'll be able to give him a much better life than he would have had if you'd still been with Trevor. Trevor was dangerous, he shouldn't be allowed to be near children or women. I know how you must feel, it's such a big day for you and you're bound to have really wanted it to go well. It must feel so disappointing for you.'

Kirsty nodded, calmer now and more in listening mode.

'I suppose I was disappointing to you,' Kirsty muttered.

I got the idea she was feeling ashamed of herself too.

'You weren't disappointing to me,' I encouraged her. The Kirsty I see before me now is quite a different person to the young woman I met a few months ago. You're stronger, wiser and more level headed than the old Kirsty. You'll be a much better mum now. That's what I can put in my report. Problems always come up in life, everyone has their ups and downs. It's how you deal with them that counts and seeing a strong young woman, determined to be a good mum is something to be proud of. Just keep going.'

I was glad to see Kirsty lifted her gaze to me briefly, eyes still tearful but at least there was the hint of a smile. She was looking up now in more ways than one.

'Anyway, I'm so sorry we got off to a difficult start,' Janet said to Kirsty, both her voice and her gaze full of warmth. 'But welcome. It's very nice to have you here and do ask for whatever you need. I find it difficult to be helpful without taking over and possibly being a bit overbearing so I try and hold back. But if I'm wrong in one way or another just tell me and I'll sort it out.'

Kirsty acknowledged the words with a brief smile.

Janet and I carried in Kirsty's few bags and let her enjoy a few moments of privacy with her son. Once the practical tasks were settled, Janet showed us Kirsty and Craig's room.

'Oh wow!' Kirsty went in first, balancing Craig on her hip. Her gaze fell on everything and it seemed like every time she turned her head something else that she liked caught her eye and she let out a little gasp of pleasure.

I wasn't surprised. The room was gorgeous. It held a cot, and a double bed plus a little single. Plenty of space for storage plus somewhere to watch TV and an armchair to sit on. There was a small bathroom and a little kitchen area big enough to cook a small meal in.

'It's great!' Kirsty jiggled a bright toy near Craig to make him laugh. He did thank goodness, she needed her confidence boosting. Mother and son were getting on well and it was lovely to see.

'Please may it last!' I prayed silently.

'I've got quite a few spare duvet covers and sheets in this cupboard.' Janet opened the door to indicate. 'I thought you'd like to choose your own. I just put that one on to start with.'

'Thank you,' Kirsty mumbled looking at the store.

'Shall we go back to the kitchen?' I asked. 'As usual there is some paperwork to do.' I pointed to a sheaf of papers from a file I had in my bag.

'Oh, boring,' Kirsty grumbled, hugging Craig close to her and gently jiggling him on her hip.

'I know, everything social services do seems to involve forms. But it's just so we agree the rules while you're here, Kirsty,' Janet explained, she was always wise and level headed. 'So there's no misunderstanding at some future date.'

I had to agree. 'Forms are boring, but if you've ever had someone complain about something it's a great help to have a written copy of what had been agreed.'

We sat around the table with some coffee and went through the form. Kirsty sat with Craig on her lap gently rocking him and and keeping him amused by giving him things to look at, a rattle, a spoon, some paper. She did follow what we were saying and added her thoughts too. I was pleased to see it, multitasking is an essential skill for every parent and it was good omen for the future of Kirsty's parenting.

'This meeting is called a Placement Planning Meeting and it sets the expectations of all the parties,' I explained for Kirsty's sake. 'We all agree on some rules then we get together and review it every so often. We might need to adjust the rules every few weeks obviously, because we're all working for your independence long term.'

I looked round at Kirsty, who seemed to have been listening and taking it all in. Satisfied with that, I moved on.

'So shall we start with who is doing what for Craig?' I asked.

'Ok. I have written a schedule to show what I do each day for Craig and roughly what time.' Janet pushed a piece of paper in Kirsty's direction. 'I want to say though that it's just a starting point. I'm sure you'll want to change it to your own way in time and that's fine by me.' Craig's hands were busily trying to grab anything so Kirsty held it high and read it.

'Ok then,' she acknowledged.

'For the first fortnight you won't take Craig out on his own as we discussed, remember? That is when the next child protection conference is, so we can discuss it then.' I looked round at Kirsty. She was looking sulky.

'But I really wanna take him to see my mates at the refuge!' she grumbled. 'Can't I even just do that?'

'You've been through such traumas and so has Craig, so you both need to be somewhere settled and to stay there for a while. That will enable you to really get to understand how to look after him. If you go out without him he will miss the chance to bond with you.'

'You don't trust me, do you?' Kirsty glared at me.

'Well, we do have to be careful, that's true. It isn't just about you but anybody who has been through the sort of trauma you and Craig have needs to rest somewhere safe,' I explained. I had to be honest even though it wasn't what Kirsty wanted to hear. 'And the people at the child protection meeting would insist on that too.'

'My mates at the refuge say you've got no right to make those rules!'

'Yes we have,' I explained patiently. 'Craig is on an Interim Care Order so that means we have shared parental responsibility for him. We don't have rights on you though. I know it's a bit much and probably it is over cautious, but when it's someone as special as little Craig we do go over the top where safety is involved. Is that ok?'

'It's gonna have to be isn't it?'

'Yes. We can talk about it at the next Child Protection Meeting in four week's time.'

'Be too late then,' Kirsty frowned.

'Are you saying you don't want to be here Kirsty?' I queried. 'Or do you just not like it?'

'I will do what you say, but no, I don't like being given so many rules,' she groaned.

'We want to give you the best chance of success,' I explained.

'I'm sorry you don't really want to be here,' Janet added helpfully. 'Your friends can come here if you like. You can use the little side sitting room. It used to be for our teenagers to use with their visitors, but of course they've all left home now.

'That's a nice offer,' I said. 'Isn't it, Kirsty?'

'S'pose.' Kirsty took a big drink of her coffee without looking at Janet. 'It's not so much being here, but being told when I can and when I can't go out.'

I thought that response from Kirsty was a bit offhand, but Janet was used to sulky teenagers and young people and she took it all in her stride. I knew that from previous work we had done together.
But what crossed my mind was Kirsty's attitude. She was already objecting and although she had said she would comply with everything asked. Was this the thin edge of the wedge? Now that she almost had Craig back, did this mean that she wanted to look after him her own way and slip back once she left Janets?

'I can see what you mean,' I spoke in soothing tones. 'But you really just need to get you and Craig established as a mother and baby team. You've lost a bit of ground together and you need to make that up. Is that ok?'

'We'll work together on it,' Janet enthused. 'Bring your friends here, we'll make a cake for them if you like.'

Kirsty looked taken aback at that, as if she hadn't made a cake before and had never considered making one for her friends. I guessed that was probably true.

'Thanks,' she replied.

Then we got on with the rest of the meeting which ran on till past the five o'clock time that I usually finished work.

It had been a difficult afternoon and staying patient with Kirsty as she objected to the care plan was hard work. Not to mention that I was also having doubts as to how her care of Craig would work out. Still, he wasn't in any danger since Janet was there but nevertheless, the care plan wasn't quite falling into place as I'd hoped. Had I done the right thing in standing up for Kirsty?

Only time would tell.

CHAPTER FOURTEEN

I left it a couple of days till contacting Kirsty or Janet to let Kirsty settle in, I was just so busy at work so it was a few days later till I rang.

'How's it going Janet?' I asked. 'The child protection conference is the week after next, and I need up to date information for my report.'

'Well, I don't really know to be quite honest. I was going to ring you because I'm a bit worried.' Janet was speaking in hushed tones, presumably Kirsty was somewhere about and she didn't want to be overheard. 'I know Kirsty hasn't been here a week yet, and at first I just thought she was tired. She has had a lot of stress plus going back to being a full time mother which must be tiring. But we don't see much of Kirsty or Craig, they are usually in their room. Kirsty does come out for meals but she takes them into her place. She comes out again to make Craig's bottles, so I know he's being fed, but that's almost all we see of them. I don't have any concerns about Craig, he seems well and happy when I do see him, but it can't be good for either of them.'

I had to agree, so I called in on my way home.

Janet showed me to Kirsty's room giving me a summary of their day's activities as we went. It did sound worrying. We needed more engagement between Janet and Kirsty for her really to get the best out of this placement. Craig would soon be starting weaning and Kirsty was bound to need advice on that.

'Hello,' I called, knocking on the door to Kirsty's room. 'It's Caz, can I come in?'

A little voice called yes and I pushed open the door, full of trepidation as to what I'd find. Kirsty and Craig were lying on the bed, which was unmade. The room looked untidy, with clothes strewn all around and coffee cups, presumably dirty, dumped on various horizontal surfaces. 'Hi,' I said as I stepped over some clothes to get to closer to Kirsty. 'It's a bit of an obstacle course in here,' I joked as I approached a chair and moved a few things so I could sit down. It might be a serious mission, but I didn't want to use a telling off tone or manner that would make Kirsty tense and anxious. I wanted her relaxed and fully engaged in thinking through a problem with me and helping to find a solution.

'How are you both?' It might well be that Kirsty was depressed, it had happened before, and the last thing she needed was judgement. I sat, waiting for her reply.

'Alright,' she said, in a lacklustre sort of way. Craig was lying next to her, kicking his feet in fun. It looked like Kirsty had been playing with him, a rattle was lying close to him. I kept my tone soft. 'Are you sure? You look a bit low and Janet says you stay in your room a lot. I worry as that is often a sign of depression.'

Kirsty dropped her gaze and picked up the rattle, pulling at the little jingly bits fixed on it absentmindedly. A tear ran down her cheek. Craig let out a screech. Having noticed his mother's attention had moved elsewhere he wanted it back. His mother looked round at him and smiled saying 'ok, poppet.' Craig smiled back at her. She picked up the rattle, shook it for him and the smile came back to his face. Craig was enjoying her shaking it for him and so was Kirsty, judging by the body language between mother and son.

I was delighted to see this spontaneous demonstration of good bonding. That was one of my questions answered. Body language says such a lot.

'You're doing so well,' I encouraged. 'I loved watching how Craig was asking you to play with him just now, he obviously likes being with you. But I asked Janet what you had been doing and she said you spend almost all your time in your room. I'm worried that you'll get depressed if you stay in here with Craig too much. Is there anything wrong?' I thought maybe some problem with something in the house perhaps.

'No,' she shook her head.

'Are you sure? Could it be a problem with someone in the house?'

Kirsty didn't answer straight away it looked like she was trying to decide how much if anything to say, but in time she spoke, quietly, timidly, meekly.

'S'pose not.'

'Hmm, that sounds like maybe there is.' I looked at her quizzically. She didn't disagree. 'Is there a problem here?'

A tear ran down her cheek but she didn't answer and wiped it quickly away. I guessed the answer to my question was yes.

'Is it with your room?'

'No,' she shook her head.

'Is it with Janet's family?'

She shook her head again, slowly. 'No.'

I was worried now. There could only be one other option, but surely not. 'Is it with Janet?' I could hardly bear to say the words. Janet was lovely, I couldn't believe she'd do anything wrong. But I must remember I was seeing her from my point of view. Kirsty was seeing her in quite another context so of course she'd have a different point of view I realised. But unless I knew what the problem was, I couldn't help fix it and my care plan would fail.

'It's Janet isn't it?'

Floods of tears ran down Kirsty's cheeks. Craig looked at her puzzled.

I dug in my bag for a tissue, I always kept a packet on me for just this sort of occasion. I passed one to her.

'I feel for you,' I sympathised. 'You've done so well, you've pulled yourself through a really difficult patch and done a great job with Craig, who obviously loves you. But something's not quite right, I can see that. What is it and I'll do my best to help?'

Craig looked over at his mum, kicked his legs and let out a huge gurgle.

'There you are,' I laughed. 'He's telling you how much he loves you.'

Kirsty looked at Craig and laughed. I laughed with her and the momentary lighter mood softened the atmosphere a little.

'What's the matter, Kirsty?' I asked softly. 'I really want to make everything right for you two. Is it something Janet said?'

'Not really…' Kirsty chocked her words out and sobbed as she spoke. 'She's had Craig ever since that day in the police station hasn't she? She must think I'm a right prat. So how can I be in the same room as her?'

Suddenly it all made sense. It's not unusual for birth parents to feel resentful of foster carers, who at that moment seemed more capable, wiser and better off financially than themselves, which they often were. At least at that time. 'I see what you mean, I think.' I never wanted to assume I was right, so I asked. 'Is it cos she looked after Craig when you couldn't?'

'Yeah. I was making his bottle in the kitchen, and she kept looking over at me. I felt like she was checking up on me all the time. So I try to only go to the kitchen when she's not there and I just get some things to eat for both of us.'

I noticed a few plates of food that had obviously been hers lying around barely touched and in need of washing up. 'Poor you!' I said. 'It is horrible thinking someone is watching what you're doing. It makes you feel like you're doing something wrong even when you're not, doesn't it?'

Kirsty nodded agreement. 'Couldn't I have gone somewhere else, with some other foster carer?'

'At the time my managers in the office were deciding whether to offer this placement to you we had to think of what was best for Craig, and obviously not moving him is best so we chose to use Janet and her family. It's not everyone who gets offered these placements you know.

But I can see, it's a very human thing and quite logical to think that about Janet but I'm sure it's not what she thinks.'

'Maybe,' Kirsty replied thoughtfully, absent-mindedly kissing the top of Craig's head at the same time.

'Would you mind if we both went to speak to her about this?' I asked. 'Only we really need to work with her so you and Craig get the best out of being here.'

Kirsty didn't answer for a few minutes, but I got the idea that now she would do anything to keep Craig, and I understood that.

'Ok then,' she muttered.

I went through the adjoining door. Janet was busily cleaning the oven. I think she had half suspected we'd need to chat so chose a job which she could easily leave and start again. Kirsty and Craig were not far behind me.

The three of us sat round the table and Kirsty sat Craig in his high chair next to her with some toys to keep him busy.

I summarised the situation for Janet. 'It feels to Kirsty like she wasn't any good for Craig when you were, which not only hurts but makes her keep away from you so you don't criticise her or think badly of her.'

'Oh you poor lass. That's not what I think at all!' Janet sounded surprised. 'I do see what you mean and I can see why you'd think that. But in fact I have the greatest admiration for you. You've had the guts to confront how you have been doing things and change. That is no easy thing to do, and I admire you for it. If I have appeared intrusive or over bossy I apologise for that. I really want to help set you and Craig up as a family forever and I'm truly sorry if I upset you.'

'Is that true?' Kirsty asked, her gaze daring to look up through her thick black eyelashes.

'Yes it is,' Janet spoke with conviction. 'I've known a lot of people, really nice people, who end up in difficult circumstances and they need just a bit of help to get back on track. I think that's what you'll be like.'

'Yeah but I chose to move in with Trev didn't I?' Kirsty sounded reserved, cautious even, as if she didn't know how much to say or not.

'You chose him because you have what is called an Attachment Disorder,' I explained. 'Because you were young and needed looking after yourself, you chose someone you thought would look after you. He probably seemed to offer all that. But at the end of the day he didn't.'

'Yeah, but that makes it my fault, doesn't it?'

'You weren't old enough to be able to judge.' Janet spoke with raw honesty, you could hear the warmth and conviction in her voice.

'Because you'd had such a hard time yourself, you didn't know what to look for. You were easy prey for anyone with slick talk and bad intentions.'

'You wouldn't criticise someone who had never had driving lessons but couldn't drive, would you? That wouldn't make sense. So why criticise someone who hadn't had the opportunity to learn about relationships because they don't understand them?' I asked.

Kirsty lifted her face. She looked a bit lighter, her head lifted a little higher.

'I could see the stress in you the first time I saw you.' Janet explained with emphasis. 'I wanted to reach out to you, to look after you, to guide you into seeing yourself the way I see you. To help you go out into the world stronger and fitter to be the person you really are inside.'

'But I'm not strong though am I? I cry all the time.' Kirsty's face dropped and she looked down again.

'Being strong isn't about not crying,' Janet said with emphasis. 'It's about being wise, being able to see when someone has a weak point and helping them learn how to overcome their difficulties and work with them. You can take that learning then and be a much wiser and more understanding person and pass that on to your own children and anyone else you meet. I just wanted to help you make good meals for Craig, manage his nappy rash, deal with his tantrums that won't be too far away, those sorts of things. You can do it. I'm sure you can.'

Kirsty didn't answer but got up and hugged Janet, who hugged her back. Tears were running down Kirsty's face. They stayed together for a few moments. It looked like Kirsty was finally making a transition that would help her long term.

Kirsty looked pale and weak. I could see how traumatised she had been. This was understandable given what she had been through. It was only too easy to end up in a difficult situation as Kirsty had, but harder to get yourself out of it.

'It's nice to see yet another hurdle being swept out of the way, Kirsty.' I added. 'And if you can let Janet look after you then that will set you up all the better to be a parent to Craig then later other children you might have.

The mood in the room changed remarkably. Kirsty was smiling, Craig was getting bored and wanted his mother's attention, so he let out a few whimpers.

'Oh no!' Kirsty said and rushed over to him, picking him up and cuddled him to her. 'What's the matter?' she asked him. 'I know. I think he's tired,' Kirsty put him in a cot kept in a corner of the kitchen where he obligingly snuggled into the soft bedding, shut his eyes and went to sleep.

'Fancy helping me bake a cake? Janet asked as Kirsty rejoined them at the table. 'I've got some chocolate drops to put in it. We can nibble a few as we go. For quality assurance testing of course!'

Kirsty laughed. 'I've never baked a cake, I always buy them at the shop.'

'You have a treat in store then,' Janet laughed, reaching some ingredients out of the cupboard. 'I always use real butter and they come out beautifully.'

I left soon after that, content that I had witnessed a change in this case and at last I was beginning to relax with Kirsty.

Things seemed to be looking up for her.

CHAPTER FIFTEEN

It was the day of the next child protection meeting. I had been round to see Kirsty with my report the day before and gone through it with her. She wasn't happy with it as she clearly told me when we were sitting on the sofa in Janet's front room.

'He don't need to be on the child protection register does he? Cos he's safe now isn't he?' Craig was whimpering in a baby chair nearby. Kirsty picked him up and held him to her, jiggling around to keep him happy.

'Yes, but that's not how the system works,' I explained, tickling Craig's chin as I did so. 'The child protection process follows you right through till the situation is properly sorted out. Hopefully for ever.'

'It can stop now,' Kirsty retorted. 'Craig is alright.'

I knew that wouldn't be acceptable, 'the members of your child protection team, won't want you to stop being on a child protection register now because you've only recently got better and you might relapse. It's too soon. They will once they see you're doing fine long term.'

Kirsty was quick to reply. 'I won't relapse, will I, cos if I do I'll loose him, won't I? Besides I love looking after him, he's my little man isn't he? I've never had anyone that stuck with me when I was a kid. I felt really lonely. Craig isn't going to have a life like that all the time I'm here.' Kirsty lifted him out of his chair and kissed him. He grinned in return, obviously delighted to be the subject of so much attention and totally familiar with it. 'And anyway, I was only like that cos of Trev, and I don't see him no more. I've told you that and you know it's true from Janet and Kurian.'

'But you're still vulnerable, and while you're still vulnerable some other awful bloke, or even woman, could groom you, because that's what they do. They convince you they're great, so they can get what they want from you and Craig. I've seen it happen.'

Kirsty couldn't object to that. That is how abusive people operate, so she huffed and took the report from me. She balanced Craig on her lap, jiggling him up and down on her knee to busy him whilst he was trying to get her attention by taking the paper from her. It was a bit of an art to keep it out of his reach whilst hanging onto the document, but she managed.

'He wants to put that in his mouth. Everything goes in his mouth.' She smiled deftly keeping the document away from Craig.

I smiled in return. He was at the age where that is exactly what he wanted to do, feel everything via his mouth. I was impressed by Kirsty's ability to recognise this and her skill in negotiating a document with a fidgety baby.

'I don't like that.' She pointed to a phrase I'd used in the report. I read the part she'd indicated. It said '...the transition in Kirsty was very welcome, but has yet to stand the test of time.'

'How can you disagree with that? It's true isn't it?' I asked, looking at her, furrowing my brow and trying to guess what she meant.

'Cos, ok, I went through a bad patch I know, but I'm out the other side now, aren't I? He doesn't need to be on any register' She turned Craig round towards her and told him that she'd be all his in a minute.

He smiled in return.

'Social services are very cautious in how they work,' I explained. 'They do move slowly because they've seen too many promising situations go wrong. But we also like our families to have a happy ending so they will back out when its time. But they'll want to know how Craig is and keep him on the register until they're really sure he'll be ok.'

'If they wanna know how Craig is, they can see how he is! It's not fair to have a meeting about him without him, so he's coming! And I am too,' she told me quite plainly.

I was shocked. Nobody has ever bought a baby to a meeting so far as I know. These events are formal and just one step down from the family court. I had to object. 'That isn't a good idea. He might start crying and distract everyone so you wouldn't be able to hear or contribute very well. I know Janet will be going so she can't babysit, but I can find another foster carer or someone at the family centre I'm sure.'

Kirsty answered in a no nonsense tone. 'No. He's going to be there and people can see how happy and well he is can't they?'

I smiled. I liked this new Kirsty. I hadn't seen the feisty side of her enough at first, argumentative yes, but feisty in the way she was defending her ability to look after Craig, no. But she was sure making up for lost time now. Part of the ability to look after herself and Craig for the rest of his childhood would be the ability to shout out to protect him if she needed too, and she was proving to be good at that. And if the child protection team had to adjust their practice somehow to allow Craig to join us, well, it wouldn't hurt them. But if Kirsty chose to interpret that as needing first hand evidence that Craig was fine, she would certainly be supplying it. I could see her point and I felt like part of her was showing off how well she was doing as a mother, which I liked.

So I rang Nitin later. He worked in a different office and I told him. He rang Kirsty on Janet's phone (no mobiles in those days). But despite Nitin's attempts to discourage her, Kirsty wouldn't change her mind. So I left it that, if need be, we could ask one of our colleagues to push Craig around in his pushchair outside the meeting room whilst we finished.

When Kirsty and Janet arrived at the meeting, with Craig in a pushchair a few days later, he was instantly the star attraction. Several of the office staff left their desks briefly to come and say hello and admire him. Kirsty and Craig were in their element. Kirsty was enjoying the attention just as much as her son.

I knew Nitin thought having a child of that age in the room was inappropriate because a child so young might distract people and if anyone has anything more difficult to say it could be harder for them. It wasn't that long ago that clients weren't allowed at all into these meetings. It was just the professionals. Then the social worker, would dash round to the parents afterwards and tell them if their child was on the 'at risk' register and why. Then it was pointed out that families would have a better understanding of their situation if they'd heard from all the professionals what the issues were, and they could challenge them if they felt that something was wrong.

So now we had a situation where all the professionals were present to discuss any concerns and offer services or ideas to put the situation right. They'd have to express their concerns or risk having the issues they worried about not addressed. It got a much better result as clients could really understand any problems and discuss how to address them.

'I ain't leaving him nowhere where I can't see him,' Kirsty announced with passion as she left the group of admiring staff to go into the meeting room. 'I've had him took off of me once and I'm not gonna let it happen again!' She took a seat in the meeting with Janet beside her and Craig in front of her. I sat on her other side. 'See, you can all look at him now and see how well he's doing.' She turned him a bit at a time to let everyone see.

People nodded in polite acknowledgement, but didn't leave their seats to welcome him.

Nitin did though. 'He certainly looks happy,' Nitin said as he crouched down to welcome Craig in person, then returned to his seat. 'If he doesn't settle well, one of our receptionists has offered to look after him outside. Is that alright?'

'S'pose,' Kirsty responded reluctantly, then addressed the whole group, with pride to describe her work with Craig. 'I do everything for him, wash and dress him and do his bottles. Don't I Janet?'

Janet nodded agreement.

It looked like we were about to start.

'Well can I thank you all for joining us today,' Nitin opened the meeting. 'And special thanks to Kirsty, who has not only taken the trouble to join us but has bought Craig to be with us too.'

It was only a small group since many issues had been resolved, there were no police, no schools yet of course, health issues were relayed by the Health Visitor.

It was Sally the Health Visitor, that I was unsure about. A bit of a tetchy person I could see she didn't like Craig being here, I saw the hard set of her lips, which didn't soften throughout the meeting. Nitin opened by saying that the police had decided not to attend and had closed the case on Kirsty. Presumably that meant that they still had work to do with Trevor, but confidentiality would have stopped them going into detail.

'Great!' Kirsty punched the air in delight on hearing that the police had closed their case on her. 'They gave me a caution, I apologised cos I can see how scary that must have been for Carey. So that's all done!'

'And I've had an apology from Dr Marianne Gladstone, she can't be with us today but she wants to see Craig again shortly and her secretary will send an appointment,' Nitin announced looking at Janet and Kirsty.

'I'll take him to see her!' Kirsty piped up. 'If my little man's gotta go somewhere then I'm going with him.'

'Great,' I explained. 'You're in charge of his health care, so you need to understand it and make sure he gets any treatment he needs.' Kirsty sat back looking satisfied. 'I will.'

At Nitin's request I summarised the changes since the last meeting and said that Kirsty didn't want Craig on the child protection register. That did not go down well with the Health Visitor. Kirsty's face fell in response.

'It's not that I don't commend you for the progress you've made,' the woman explained. 'That is impressive and well done you. Your care of Craig is excellent, we can all see that. It's just that risking your baby's life as you did is such a big thing, I want to be thoroughly assured that you're not going to do that again. So I think he needs to remain on the child protection register for the time being.'

'I see what you mean,' others added. 'It is early days yet, we don't want to take away the protective factors too soon.'

I could see Kirsty's bubble burst, her whole expression fell and she replied in fury, her eyes welling up with tears. 'But I never was gonna to throw him! How can you say that? You don't trust me and I can't even take him out on my own!'

'I think we could have a quick tally to see if we're all happy to change that so you can go out alone. After all you've been with Janet two weeks now, and are doing well.'

Hazel from the family centre lifted her hand and added, 'if you can take Craig out, you can bring him to see us.'

Graham counted the others, who had done likewise. 'That's unanimous. We all agree so you can go out alone now with Craig. But I'm less sure of taking Craig off the register just yet.'

'I agree,' said the person from the fostering team. 'The register does offer some protection and I've always thought making change slowly was the best plan. It would be too easy to slip up if we take support away too quickly.'

I could see both points of view. I generally took a very cautious approach to the children in my care and was just framing my answer.

'It is true,' Trish interjected, 'that we have no clear evidence Kirsty did intend to throw Craig. Indeed the psychologists report does say otherwise. But nobody can be really sure.'

'I didn't! I didn't!' Tears fell fast from Kirsty's eyes thick and fast.

'You can see how well he is! Look! Look! For goodness sake!'

'Hey, Kirsty.' Unusually for me I laid my hand on her forearm in support. I generally don't touch clients because so many had been sexually abused. The last thing I'd want to do was intrude on their space. But I didn't think that was the case with Kirsty. 'Nobody's saying you haven't done well, you have and it's brilliant the way you've turned your and Craig's lives around. All people are saying is just take a little bit longer to get both your recovery really, really well set up. And if your progress is still as fab as it has been, we won't object.'

Kirsty listened intently to what I was saying, then she looked around at each of the group members to see if they were in agreement. They each replied in turn, either nodding or simply saying 'yes'. I could see that Kirsty listened, though she gave a big sigh, and was resigned to the plan.

'It won't be for long,' I added. Just a few more weeks if you keep up this progress. Then you'll never have to see any of us again!' I laughed. 'I meant that in the nicest possible way!'

Everyone else joined in and a chorus of chuckles echoed around the room.

Kirsty joined in too. It was a rare moment in what is a very formal meeting in which you could enhance the smooth passage of a care plan without detracting from it by lightening the mood a little. However you dress it up, everyone wanted Craig to still be subject to a child protection plan and like it or not Kirsty would have to go along with that.

'I s'pose I'm going to have to aren't I?' Craig giggled as she spoke.

'And even he thinks too!' I laughed, and everyone joined in.

'So we'll see you at the Family Centre then?' Hazel asked.

'Will do,' Kirsty agreed.

'Well I guess that means we can bring this meeting to an end.' Nitin looked around at the group members. 'Do I take it we still want Craig's name to remain on the child protection register?'

All agreed and the meeting ended.

CHAPTER SIXTEEN

I was sure now Craig was safe with his mother, so I rang the housing department and asked them to look for a place for mother and son. They have an agreement with us at social services that they would give some of our clients priority in housing. There was no point in working with someone only for them to end up in substandard housing and risk going right back to the beginning again.

After that I spent more and more time on other clients who were still in crisis. It was about a fortnight later that I saw Kirsty and Craig again but I had heard good reports from Janet and Hazel who had seen them so I knew there was nothing to worry about there.

It just so happened that I had to go to the hospital to see someone else at the same time that Craig was seeing Dr Gladstone The consultants secretaries usually send social workers notification of these appointments when a child is subject to a legal order of some sort. The visit I was at before this had just finished so I thought I'd make my way along to Dr Gladstone's consulting room and meet Kirsty and Craig there.

Kirsty saw me as soon as I entered the waiting room.

'Oh hi.' She looked surprised to see me and greeted me in a wary tone of voice. 'What are you doing here?'

I guess it's right that she would be wary of seeing me unexpectedly when I'd already taken Craig away from her once. 'It's ok,' I reassured her. 'I'm not here for anything in particular. I was just in the hospital seeing someone else and thought I'd pop along and join you two with the doctor. That is if you don't mind,' I added quickly. The issue of whether Kirsty minds or not isn't quite relevant. If the local authority have an interim care order on a child as we had on Craig then we have shared parental responsibility and can attend jointly if we wanted to. But since it looked like we'd be rescinding our application for a care order because Kirsty and Craig were doing so well, it was only polite to ask.

'Alright by me,' Kirsty answered, sounding a bit miffed.

The department was quiet. We were being seen outside usual clinic times. These appointments can then be adapted to suit the family's needs. Some parents need extra time to understand what they're told, parents or children can kick off if they're stressed in any way, they're not ordinary consultations.

It didn't take long till Dr Gladstone's door was opened and we were invited in. The doctor greeted me by name since we'd worked together on different cases quite a few times.

'You probably won't have met Craig's mum yet have you?' I enquired and introducing Kirsty at the same time. 'I think Janet brought him last time if I remember rightly.'

'That's right,' the doctor replied with warmth. 'Nice to meet you Kirsty.'

'You've probably read the minutes of the case conference, but Kirsty is now in a mother and baby placement with Craig. She's resolved a lot of the problems she had when first she came to our attention and she wants to learn to look after him herself now. She's doing well.' I said to update the doctor.

The doctor gave Kirsty a warm smile. 'Good for you. Now, let's see how you are young man shall we? If you wouldn't mind undressing him please.'

Kirsty bent down, unclipped Craig's safety straps on his pushchair and lifted him to the waiting couch, quickly taking his clothes off.

'Well, you do look at lot heavier than when I first met you,' the doctor announced, reaching forward to lift him onto the weighing scales. Craig screamed the moment she touched him and he looked for his mother, holding his arms out towards her.

'Oh you poor little chap! I guess I am a stranger to him,' the doctor soothed. 'Would you mind lifting him onto the scales, please Kirsty?' Kirsty lifted Craig onto the scales where he was weighed then returned to the couch, for his full examination. He was still looking around himself with concern. He didn't seem to like being separated from his mum, but he let the doctor do her tests with his mum standing close to him.

It was then that I realised the bond between mother and child was now very strong and we'd have to discuss in the child protection meeting whether this care order was now in Craig's best interests because it looked to me like it was entirely unnecessary, which was a great accolade for Kirsty and the work we had all done with the family.

It took a good few minutes till the doctor had finished. Kirsty stood by looking nervously on and watching the doctor's every move.

Eventually she announced her verdict, moving her stethoscope from her ears. 'I'm pleased to announce that if Craig had any developmental delays or health issues they have now been resolved. He is as fit and healthy as any other young man his own age,' she announced with a smile.

'Oh wow, brilliant!' Kirsty did a little dance on the spot and Craig laughed. I guessed he'd seen this little game before. 'So you don't need that care order, do you?"

'I'm just one of a team,' I explained. 'So I can't speak for us all. But I don't see that we have grounds for it anymore. It's obviously something we need to talk about as a group, but I think you've completely turned both of your lives around for the better. I wouldn't want to stop the support you're getting, both from Janet and the family centre straight away, but it is looking good long term.'

' That is fantastic!' Kirsty returned Craig to his pushchair and left the room, all the time chatting away to her son.

'Well, that looks like a good job, well done,' Dr Gladstone said.

'It certainly does,' I concluded. 'I wish they all ended that way.'

The following morning I had supervision with Trish and Graham. We spoke about Kirsty.

'She's done a great job,' I explained. 'Craig relates to her really well, he smiles when he sees her and looks to her for protection like when she was with Marianne and she put him on the cold weighing scales. He screamed and held out his arms to his mum. It was really sweet to watch. Marianne said he was now over his problems of a few months ago and has put on weight nicely. She says his development is now normal for a child of his age.

Staff at the family centre are really pleased with mother and baby. Kirsty takes Craig twice a week, always uses the staff as well as Janet to teach her all the little things you need to know about babies, weaning, sleeping, nappy problems and all sorts. Apparently she's made a couple of friends there now who have babies of similar ages. Reports are good. Kirsty has bonded with Craig and he with her.'

My managers had listened with great concentration all the way through to everything I said, Trish sitting back thoughtfully with her arms folded in front of her, Graham sat forward, hands on his thighs, looking down as he often did at times of great concentration.

They sat back into thoughtful mode once I'd finished.

Trish was first to speak. 'It all sounds very promising doesn't it?'

'It does,' Graham agreed.

'We need a child protection meeting and if everyone agrees we can deregister the family.'

'When is the next meeting?' Graham asked.

'Its another two months. And Kirsty is really keen that we don't have Craig's name on the register any longer than we need to.'

'And she's got a point,' Graham added. 'It is very unethical to have someone's name on the register any longer than necessary.'

'Caz, why don't you ring Nitin?' Trish suggested. 'Explain everything to him and ask if he agrees with us bringing the meeting forward. Then it's his secretary's job to find a date that suits everyone and send the invitations out.'

'Great!' I said, jotting down notes in my diary on my things to do list.

'If the meeting agrees,' Trish said, 'we'll need to let the legal department know. They'll update the court. It may well be that we no longer have grounds for a care order anyway.'

Thinking they'd finished, I got up to leave the room, but I was called back.

'Oh Caz,' Graham called. 'Ring the housing department to make sure they have a place for them to live when they leave Janet's.'

'Done the housing. Thanks, both,' I replied in a hurry. My heart was singing, but at the same time I was nervous. What if I had got it wrong and misled Kirsty? What if Kirsty was just putting on an act? I doubted it the logical part of my brain told me. She'd been consistent in all her care of Craig and her lifestyle since she separated from Trevor.

There was every reason to believe that the transformation was permanent.

It was not until later that week that I had the date finalised for the next child protection conference and my next report was finished for Kirsty to read in a file. I popped round on my way home from work so that she could read it and I could give her the new date and time.

The door was opened by Janet who explained that Kirsty was in the garden with a couple of friends. She showed me through to the garden where Kirsty and two other women were sitting on the lawn, chatting. There were two small children as well as Craig of course, one who could walk and one who couldn't who was pulling himself up with the help of one of the women, presumably his mother. There was lots of chatting and giggling going on and it seemed a happy event. Kirsty looked up when she saw me, her face fell and went pale.

There was such a lot of power in my job. It's easy to forget that. but just to look at Kirsty was proof. She wouldn't know just yet the real reason for my visit so I guess being scared made sense.

She turned to her friends, said something, then ran up to the backdoor where Janet and I were standing.

'Could I just have a word?' I asked, holding my file up by way of explanation. I couldn't talk to her with her friends present because of confidentiality, obviously.

'Why don't you go in the study?' Janet suggested. 'You'll be private in there. I'll watch Craig for you.'

'Ok then.' I followed Kirsty who took us into a little room with a desk and a couple of chairs. I took one, Kirsty the other.

'It's nothing to worry about,' I explained. I didn't want to be too upbeat, after all the meeting might decide to keep Craig's name on the register so I couldn't jump to conclusions. 'But I have managed to move the next child protection meeting forward to next Tuesday and I have the file here for you to read my report.'

'Oh!' Kirsty gasped and took the file.

'Just read the conclusion if you can only spare a few minutes,' I explained. 'That will give you the gist of it and you can read the detail later.'

With a wary look on her face Kirsty took the document, scanned through to the end, then read it. It wasn't too long till her face beamed with pride.

Kirsty read out loud, '…so you recommend that Craig's name be taken off the register and the care plan we created moved on so that Kirsty and Craig can move out of Janet's and into a house already identified for them via the local housing association. A care team at the family centre should be identified for them both to give ongoing support and the court approached to rescind our application for a care order…'

'Wow!' she screamed jumping up from her chair and putting her arms round my neck in a bear hug. 'Caz, that is brilliant!'

In a nano second she had opened the door, retraced her steps to the garden and shouted out the conclusion of the report to the others, waving it in the air by way of explanation.

'Guess what?' she called. 'Craig's name is going to be taken off the register!"

'Well, maybe,' I explained. 'It's not only my decision remember, I'm just one of a team. But it is my recommendation.' My explanation fell on deaf ears and Kirsty danced around the garden in delight. Since the chances of the end of the interim order was high, I didn't remind her about it she was so excited, so I said my goodbyes and went on my way home.

It was only a few days till the day of the child protection conference. Kirsty had again chosen to bring Craig 'I'm not leaving him out of his own meeting!' she insisted so yet again I had to ask one of the admin team if they could step in if the baby got fractious and they were all delighted. They love babies!

'It sounds like we have good news from the social worker who has been looking after mother and son. Carey proposes that we deregister Craig because of the couple's good progress,' Nitin said by way of introduction. 'Let's go round the room and ask all attendees for their up to date views on the two. Hazel from the Family centre, would you like to go first?'

'Yes,' Hazel cleared her throat. 'Kirsty has been coming both to our drop in sessions and our Friday under Five's group where the parents, usually mothers, bring their children, have a cup of tea and get their babies weighed and speak to the Health Visitor about any worries or concerns they may have on just about anything really. Sometimes we also have a social worker present too, Carey often comes, and she can help with other issues, family problems, housing, that sort of thing. It's developed into quite a close group of people, about four or five of them really get on well and have started meeting up outside the centre. It's been great for Kirsty especially, as the families she's made friends with have children just a little bit older than her, so she's had a little glimpse of future child development. They're a nice, steady group of friends who have helped Kirsty grow into the sensible, caring mum she now is, so yes, I'm in favour of Carey's proposal.'

'That's good to hear.' Nitin acknowledged. 'Sally?' Nitin looked at the Health Visitor.

'Things have changed a lot since our last meeting,' the Health Visitor said. 'I've been seeing Kirsty at the family centre. She is taking a lot of interest in the different groups there and has been learning a lot. Craig has come on well too, I'm no longer concerned about him so yes, he no longer needs our protection.'

'Thank you, that sounds very positive,' Nitin said. 'Janet, how about you?'

'I can only say the same thing,' Janet explained. 'Kirsty was committed from the first. I think she felt suffocated having a boyfriend. I won't use the word partner because he didn't behave like a partner. He totally put himself first all the time. He would demand what he wanted, when he wanted it with no consideration for anyone else, not even Craig and Kirsty. I think she got swamped in a downward spiral of negativity and abuse and couldn't see a way out.'

'People often do that don't they? I said forgetting it wasn't my turn to speak. 'They completely loose confidence in themselves and their ability to make decisions.'

'Yes, Graham agreed. 'Quite often it helps to make the decision for them. By taking their child away you jolt them into action, either they have to fight for their family or go their own separate ways.'

'I totally accept that sometimes parenthood isn't for everyone,' Trish elaborated. 'The demands of babies are round the clock and exhausting. I always feel sympathy with parents who struggle. Life with children isn't easy, especially if you're on a budget.'

'Hear, hear,' Nitin echoed. 'Nothing about parenting is easy, and for people with few resources life is much more difficult. Caz, can we hear from you next?'

I gave my report, much as I'd already outlined, with one addition. 'There is no hurry for them to move out of Janet's, but she has been there almost three months and we do have pressure to use the placement for others. Thanks to Janet's wonderful guidance, Kirsty no longer needs Janet's help. I think that for Craig and his mother's future we would like to see the couple continuing to go to the family centre. Kirsty has already agreed to that. That means if there are any future concerns the family centre can always re-refer to us again. What is new, and it's so new I haven't even told Kirsty yet, is that the housing department have identified a property that they think they may be able to make available to mother and son. It's on Lilac Way.' I glanced over at Kirsty, I didn't want her to get too excited so I addressed my final comment to her. 'I haven't mentioned it before because it's not certain, so don't get too excited yet.'

'Oh wow,' Kirsty looked hopeful.

'Thank you for that update, Caz.' Nitin turned to his fellow meeting attendees and asked. 'Could we have a show of hands as to who thinks we no longer need Craig on the Child Protection Register?'

I looked round at Kirsty. She was looking tense. But she needn't have done, all the votes went in her favour. But Kirsty knew that wasn't quite the end of it.

'Thank you,' Nitin announced again. 'Now who is in agreement with Craig no longer being subject to an Interim Care Order and our application to the Family Court to rescind our application be invoked.' Nitin and Kirsty scanned the room again, Kirsty looked even more tense and nervous. But all hands went up, all were in favour of the removal of the Interim Care Order!

Kirsty leapt out of her chair and danced around in delight.

People started clapping. 'Well done Kirsty! You've really turned two lives around!' The health visitor said.

The mood in the room was elated. That sort of success makes the job such a special job. 'You've done brilliantly!' I said.

CHAPTER SEVENTEEN

It was about a week later before I saw Kirsty and Craig again. They'd come into the office to find out if there was any news about housing. By chance, I'd just had news myself.

'You're in luck,' I stated as we sat in one of the little side rooms that not so long ago had been the scene of such sadness for Kirsty. 'As it happens, we can pick up the keys tomorrow and you can move in straight away.'

Kirsty yelped with happiness. 'But what about furniture?'

'I thought you'd ask that. We can make a grant available to you to buy a cooker and fridge, secondhand but safety checked, and there are charities that can help with furniture. Carpets and flooring are already in place. There is a local charity that has a big warehouse full of clothes and furniture for people in need. It's like a huge treasure chest of all things all lovely, fresh and clean. Fancy going now?' Luckily, I had some free time.

'Oh yes please!' Kirsty turned to Craig. 'Did you hear that? We can go and choose some things for your new bedroom!'

Of course Craig didn't have enough language skills to know what he was being told, but he got the idea that whatever his mother said was good and very exciting and he grinned from ear to ear. He was so happy these days, it was a delight to see mother and son together. He might be only eight months old now, but he had such a lot of personality and a real little twinkle in his eyes. He'd break a few hearts when he was older, I thought.

That's why I love social work, you might only know someone a few months or a year or so, but you're often with them at the most intense and difficult period of their lives and being able to support them through that is so rewarding.

'They can usually deliver whatever you want over the next few days and you can move in at the weekend? I can ask some volunteers to help with lifting things if you like?'

'Even better!'

'Come on then, let's go!'

A short while later we were at the storage depot, actually a large room at the side of a local factory which had an element of warmth to it so nothing was damp.

'Welcome!' said a cheery man as we entered. 'You're the social worker who rang a little while ago I take it? You faxed through the paperwork just now?'

'Yes,' I replied. 'This is Kirsty and I am Caz. And this is Craig. They're about to move into their first flat ever so need everything.'

'Right you are then. I hope you didn't mind me checking, only we get some lovely things given by the local church. If I wasn't so careful who comes in here I'd get all the local dealers coming round to help themselves.'

'I bet. There are some cheeky types about,' I looked around at the store.

'C'mon then. Let's get you started.' He pointed to each group of items as he spoke. 'Over there are beds, then you'll see sofa's, chairs, sideboards, bedroom furniture in that direction.' He waved his hand to indicate. 'Then over there is all the equipment you could want, saucepans, plates and things, and just to finish it off, some clothes, duvet covers and fabric stuff over there.'

'Wow!' Kirsty looked around her in delight.

'Off you go and get stuck in.' Our assistant waved us in, a broad smile on his lips and a generous manner. 'Basically, if you can't see what you want, ask. Because if we haven't got it, we can probably get it.'

'Thanks!' Kirsty was off, pushing Craig in his buggy, her eyes wide open with excitement. And I followed behind, enjoying seeing Kirsty so happy and with such a great future.

'Look at these beds Caz…and look! Look at that one!' She scrambled through a narrow gap in some beds to one that was up against the rear wall. 'Look! It's a fire engine made into a bed!'

I looked over to it, It had a little 'cab' over the pillow area with a little brass bell hanging over the middle. 'Kirsty that is gorgeous! The assistant helped us get it out, so we could see it properly.

'How lovely! That'd be brilliant. I know he has to have a cot until he's a bit bigger, but that will come soon.'

'It certainly will,' I agreed. 'Now how about a bed for you?' Reserving the fireman's bed we went to the adults' bed area. Very soon we had a collection of lovely things all put to one side for Kirsty, and even some lovely duvet covers and towels too.

'I'm gonna ring Nat and Jo. They can come round and help me get set up. They said they've been looking forward to that for a long time. Jo said she furnished her whole house with charity shop furniture for less than £250.'

'She sounds a canny lass,' I laughed.

Kirsty steered Craig towards the door and left without a backwards glance but something about her had changed. I sat and pondered what it was, then it came to me. There was a new tone in her voice, a new confidence, a sense of freedom, of maturity, that I'd never heard from her before. It was heartwarming.

'We have a large waiting list of people waiting for a social worker,' Graham told me in supervision.

I knew what was coming next, and it made me sad and exhilarated in equal measure.

'Trish and I think you should do one more visit to Kirsty and Craig in their new place then leave the family centre to monitor them. We need everyone to be working at their maximum for those on the waiting list.'

'I see what you mean. I'll miss Kirsty and Craig though.'

'You do get attached to people you've helped, and you have done very well with them. We were looking at a child in care and a possible adoption. That would be very expensive in both emotional and financial costs.'

'It wasn't the money I was thinking about,' I replied. 'But the human situation. I totally get that some parents, for whatever reason, are not able to bring up their children. But with Kirsty something niggled me, something told me that she wasn't one of them. She'd just totally lost her way and needed pulling out.'

'That's exactly right.' Graham looked at me. 'You did very well to recognise it. Some people get an idea and just plough forward without taking all the circumstances into account, or any change in circumstances, into consideration.'

'Ah, this sounds like the sort of pep talk you give when you're wanting staff to take on some other very tricky case,' I joked.

'Well, funny you should say that,' Graham laughed. 'I do have one or two in mind, but for today, pop and say goodbye to Kirsty and let her know if she has any more concerns and the family centre can't deal with them, then she's to ring the duty desk here or yourself.'

'I will do.' I gathered my notebook and went back to my desk.

I was bittersweet as I walked up to Kirsty's front door for the first and last time. She'd come a long way since I met her and part of me was sad I probably wouldn't be seeing her again.

She was expecting me this time and opened the door with a cheery welcome.

'Come in,' she called as she stood aside. She was holding Craig, who recognised me and smiled as I entered, I held his hand and gave him a cheery greeting.

'It's looking like a home already!' I said as I looked around me. 'How long have you been here?'

'Three days. Jo and Nat have helped. 'Come and see what we've done already. We'll go into Craig's room first.'

'Oh it's lovely!' I said as I stepped over the threshold. A brightly coloured mobile hung above a chest of drawers with a changing mat on it, a cot with a jolly duvet and loads of soft toys gathered at one end looked welcoming. The fireman's bed was set up ready in a corner. A brightly coloured cupboard with drawers underneath stood on the other side of the room, making the whole place a kiddies paradise.

'I painted that,' Kirsty pointed to the brightest colour cupboard.

'Did you?' I turned to look at it. It even had Craig's name painted on the side in contrasting colours. 'How gorgeous! Does he sleep well in there?'

'Yes, he always sleeps well.'

'You're lucky,' I replied. I knew plenty of babies who didn't and the stress it puts on their families is phenomenal.

We went along to Kirsty's room. The door was shut.

'I shut the door because it's still a bit of a mess in there,' Kirsty explained.

'It takes a while once you move in to get places sorted out doesn't it?' I sympathised.

The bathroom was tiny but clean and neat. The kitchen had a little table and chairs, with the addition of a high chair. Boxes of breakfast cereal stood on the work surface next to a shiny new kettle. Some leaflets, probably from the family centre, about good diet lay on the table. These things are music to a social worker's ear because it means the occupants of the house are eating well, which is always a good thing.

Kirsty made me a coffee and we took our drinks to the sitting room. I sat on a sofa that was a little dated but still comfy and Kirsty sat on a large armchair that again had been well used but had enough life left in it to make it useful. A basket of children's toys sat at the side of the room. A blanket lay on the floor and Kirsty put Craig on it with a few toys around him. He deftly turned from his back to his tummy and lifted his chest to see the things that had been laid out for him.

The whole property had an air of warmth and cosiness about it that made it a nice place to visit.

We chatted a little about what it was like living in her own home. It was nice to hear that some of the friends she had made at the Refuge and Family centre had all rallied round and found things to help with. It seemed they had the same confidence in her that I did.

Finally it was time to go. 'You'll be pleased to hear I don't need to come and see you anymore,' I explained. 'You'll be seeing the people at the family centre and they can help with any problems if you need them.'

'Thank you,' she muttered. 'Thank you. You believed in me when I hardly believed in myself. I'm - we're grateful to you for that.'

I stood and walked towards the door.

'That's no problem,' I replied. 'Anyone would have been depressed after going through what you went through.'

And with that I left. It was nice to have been thanked, but hardly necessary. It was my job and I wouldn't have it any other way.

Epilogue

It was a few years before I saw Kirsty and Craig again in a local park. It was summer and I was taking a short cut to my next visit. The area was busy with shoppers, parents and children, especially near the play area. I thought nothing of it until one young man ran across the path in front of me. There was something familiar about him but at first I wasn't sure why.

Another child followed him, presumably it was a game of chase. 'Craig!' his friend called out him.

Craig! Of course he was! His lovely brown eyes were the same. The change was dramatic, but then it would be since he was still in nappies when I last saw him and of course there was no chance he'd recognise me..

He looked in my direction but seemed to be involved in a game of chase that ended in huge bursts of giggles until the lad he was playing with fell and let out an almighty scream.

But then my guess was confirmed. Kirsty ran over with the mother of the other child. Her hair was shorter and her body looked a little more full, less youthful. But she seemed to have a confidence and poise that was just beginning when I last saw her.

She bent down to Craig's level and seemed to be explaining something to him, probably the need not to run so fast. At one point she looked straight in my direction. I was sure she saw me. But she carried on speaking to her son.

I said nothing. I didn't wave or make any sign of recognition at all. For some parents the time they had with social workers bought up memories of a different time, a time when they had been low and it seemed that the whole world was caving in on them. A time they'd rather forget.

She was with friends too, to have said hello would mean letting them know that Kirsty had once been low enough to have a social worker. If she had acknowledged me first I would have been happy to say hello and stop and have a chat with her, but she didn't.

Whether she remembered me or not at that moment was debatable. But what I could see was that Craig looked like a lively, happy young man. There was none of the downcast expression, the dull tone to the skin and eyes that you often see with children who are having a hard time. Craig looked as bright as a button, as we used to say, and his mother the same, older, wiser more self composed.

I had no role in their lives anymore and that was for the best. But there was a family that did need my help that Graham had ready for me and I hoped I could bring about a similar outcome.

I looked away and increased my pace. There are always more people needing our help.

I'd better do my best to get on.

Printed in Great Britain
by Amazon

21721665R00078